MILITARY
IMPROVISATIONS
During the
RUSSIAN CAMPAIGN

PREFACE

This pamphlet was prepared for the Historical Division, European Command, by a group of former German generals and general staff officers. The names of the contributors are not announced at this time. The principal author, who by the end of the war had attained the rank of full general *(Generaloberst)*, served on the Eastern Front throughout the Russian campaign and the subsequent retreat into the northern plains of Germany. He was successively commander of an infantry brigade, of a panzer division from November 1941 to February 1943, and of two different corps in the battles for Kharkov and Belgorod during 1943. Appointed commander of a panzer army on 1 December 1943, he participated in the withdrawal in the south until the Germans reached the Carpathians. In August 1944 he was transferred to Army Group Center, and his last assignment was with Army Group Weichsel. During this final phase of his military career he played an important part in the retreat from Lithuania, East Prussia, and Pomerania.

The reader is reminded that all publications in the GERMAN REPORT SERIES were written by Germans from the German point of view and that the procedures of the German Army differed considerably from those of the United States Army. Authorized German tables of organization and equipment, official German combat doctrine, or standard German staff methods form the basis for improvisations throughout this pamphlet. As prepared by the authors, this study consisted of a collection of 157 examples of improvisations which were screened by the editors for pertinence, clarity, and interest to the American reader. Moreover, an attempt was made to establish common denominators for the great variety of examples. Although the manuscript was completely reorganized during this editorial process, every effort was made to retain the point of view, the expressions, and even the prejudices of the authors.

CONTENTS

MAPS

Note.   Numbered maps are in sequence after page 104.

Map No.

1.   6th Panzer Division (22 June 1941—20 January 1942).

2.   The Snail Offensive (End of January to Beginning of April 1942).

3.   Operation SEYDLITZ (Situation on 3 July 1942, the Second Day of the Attack).

4.   Improvisations in East Prussia.

5.   Corduroy Roads in the Leningrad Area.

6.   The Withdrawal Across the Dnepr.

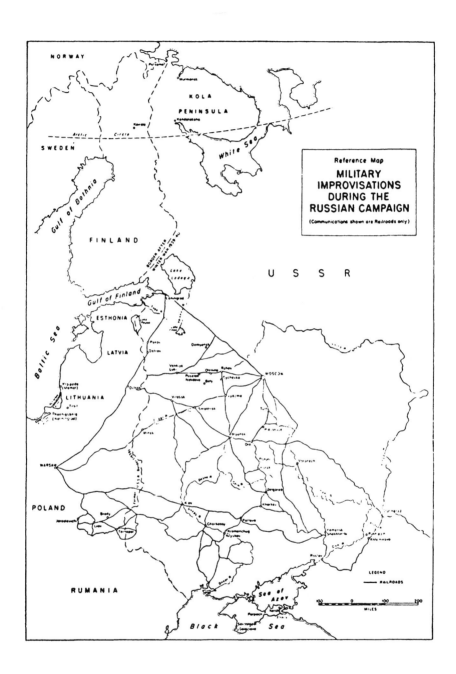

Reference Map

**MILITARY
IMPROVISATIONS
DURING THE
RUSSIAN CAMPAIGN**

(Communications shown are Railroads only)

LEGEND

——— RAILROADS

PART ONE

INTRODUCTION

The art of war involves the correct estimation and careful weighing of one's own as well as the enemy's capabilities and is marked by the conduct of military operations in a manner promising the highest degree of success. Success in war can be achieved only if the military commander employs his resources with correct timing in suitable terrain and in a way that guarantees maximum effect.

The conduct of war is subject to the same imperfections and frailties as any other field of human endeavor; for this reason emergencies which, of necessity, lead to improvisations arise from time to time in every war and in every army. Faulty planning, unsatisfactory performance of matériel, and violations of basic principles of warfare cause deficiencies which can be alleviated through improvisation but can only be overcome by sacrificing time, space, and strength. Blunders are made in every military sphere, in all places, and on the highest as well as on the lowest level. No wonder that such blunders, oversights, and frictions entail improvisations of all types, from the simplest to the most elaborate, from the strictly temporary to the chronic.

By dint of its long duration and ever-widening scope, World War II created a persistent state of deficiencies in the German Army which forced the military agencies to introduce a multitude of improvisations of all types. Insufficiently prepared for the campaign in the East, for example, the Army was faced with a great calamity as early as the muddy period and winter of 1941–42. Top-level staffs and field forces alike were forced to improvise extensively. As the campaign wore on and the German military potential continued to decline, improvisations of the widest variety became increasingly prevalent. Toward the end of the war the ratio of strength between the German and Russian Armies became so disproportionate that improvisations, especially in combat operations, were rampant. Finally, the entire conduct of war was one great improvisation.

1

The present study lays no claim to comprehensiveness, but even this fragmentary account may show the main characteristics of German improvisations and the part they played in military operations. The many separate examples are presented along functional lines, and the material is subdivided into tactical, logistical, technical, and organizational improvisations. Other bases could have been adopted. Some readers may be interested in analyzing the German improvisations in terms of their causes, or of their inevitability, or even chronologically as indicators of the extremes to which an army fighting Soviet Russia was put.

PART TWO

TACTICAL IMPROVISATIONS

As the pillar of Germany's military might, the Army had to bear the brunt of the fighting during World War II. The heartbeat of the Army was at the front, where deficiencies and shortages of any kind were immediately felt. Improvisations and expedients introduced at the front had to show quick results because, in the face of the enemy, time was of the essence. With the territorial expansion of the war, tactical commanders frequently became responsible for areas that they were unable to control with the troops and matériel at their disposal. Resources were particularly taxed whenever the forces suffered heavy casualties for which replacements could not be expected to arrive for a long time. High and low echelons alike were therefore very often forced to introduce improvisations to solve their problems as well as possible. Their efforts were concentrated on three types of tactical improvisations—the formation and commitment of combat staffs and units in sudden critical situations, the employment of units for missions outside their normal scope, and the adaptation of tactics to unexpected situations. A combination of two or more tactical improvisations had to be introduced in many cases.

Chapter 1

The Offensive

I. The Elimination of Russian Forces in a German Rear Area

1. *The Blitzkrieg Bogged Down in Mud* (Map 1)

On 22 June 1941 the 6th Panzer Division moved out of the Tilsit area as part of a provisional panzer army. In true blitzkrieg manner it rolled across Lithuania and Latvia within a few days, overran every enemy position in its way, broke through the Stalin Line, crossed the Dvina River, and opened the gateway to Leningrad on the Luga River—all within three weeks from its day of departure. This 500-mile trip led through dust and sand, woods and swamps, and across rivers and antitank ditches. Leningrad was within sight.

3

At this very time the division was called upon to assume the leading part in the German attack on the central front. Once again the division moved with lightning speed and covered 600 miles to join Army Group Center. On 10 October 1941, the first day of the offensive, its 260 tanks made a deep penetration into the enemy lines near Vyazma. Ten days later the Russians were encircled and the mission was accomplished.

The 6th Panzer Division was then to lead the attack on Moscow and take the city. Its spearheads were approaching the objective when nature suddenly put a protective wall around the Russian capital. The autumn mud brought the blitzkrieg to a sudden end. It swallowed the most valuable equipment. The cold winter continued the terrible destruction. Then came the German withdrawal during which every tank, every antitank gun, and almost every artillery piece of the division had to be sacrificed. Enemy attacks and cold weather caused innumerable casualties during rear guard actions. When the once-proud 6th Panzer Division finally assembled its forces in January 1942, all that remained were 57 riflemen, 20 engineers, and 3 guns.

After this terrible hemorrhage the remaining staffs and the supply and rear elements were assembled forty miles behind the front line for the purpose of reorganizing the division. Every day a few tankers, artillery men, and others who had escaped the carnage trickled back to the divisional area. As soon as they arrived they had to help guard the highway and railroad between Smolensk and Vyazma, the life lines of Fourth and Ninth Armies, against attacks by Russian cavalry, parachute troops, and partisans who had penetrated deep into the rear areas. The enemy first advanced southward and then turned east toward the railroad and highway connecting Vyazma with Rzhev in order to cut off the supply of Ninth Army. The field hospitals and motor pools of several divisions were under attack, and two airfields were in immediate danger. Far and wide no combat troops were available. The over-all situation did not permit the release of even the few remnants of 6th Panzer Division to serve as cadre for an alert unit which was to be improvised in the rear. By the end of January 1942 the situation was so tense that Marshal Stalin felt justified in announcing the impending annihilation of two German armies in the biggest battle of encirclement in history. But events were to develop differently.

2. *Desperate Improvisations*

Emergency alert units had to be improvised and committed immediately even though no combat cadres were available. Actually the 6th Panzer Division had not the necessary service personnel to organize even one such unit. Ninth Army therefore issued orders that the division assemble immediately all the service and supply units, as well as construction and roadbuilding battalions in the army rear area, and intercept all stragglers. Between Sychevka and Vyazma a defensive front was to be built up in the most expeditious manner. (Map 2) Even the Luftwaffe units at the Novo-Dugino airfield were subordinated to the division commander for use in ground combat.

Within twenty-four hours the staffs of all units now subordinate to 6th Panzer Division were busy intercepting every available officer and man in their respective areas and forming emergency alert units of varied strength and composition. Special care was taken that men from the same unit remained together. Depending on their number, they formed squads, platoons, or companies under the command of their former officers. Whenever possible emergency alert units of similar composition were organized into battalions and two or more battalions were placed under the command of one of the previously mentioned staffs. Each unit was to keep the weapons and supplies it had salvaged from its parent unit. This procedure was a guarantee against unnecessary splitting up of available manpower and resources. It seemed a better policy to commit units of differing strength and composition rather than to destroy unit integrity by equalizing numbers. The strength and composition of individual units was taken into account in the assignment of defense sectors.

Most men were armed with rifles. Each company had one or two machine guns, and some of the battalions had a few mortars and small antitank guns which had been procured from ordnance shops in the vicinity. Initially only one recently repaired artillery piece was available, but the flow of weapons and equipment improved daily because the maintenance and repair shops made a maximum effort to send matériel to the front. Numerous convalescents and men returning from furlough were employed along the rapidly forming front facing west.

The newly formed units had to be committed without delay wherever the danger was greatest. Frequently this baptism occurred on the very day of their initial organization. If possible, the alert units were committed in a sector where they could protect their own service and rear installations, a task with which they were only too glad to comply. For the same reason Luftwaffe units were assigned to the defense sectors that covered their own airfields. The remaining gaps were closed by alert units which had their assembly area farther away from the new front.

The most important sectors of the forty-mile front were occupied on the first day, gaps were filled in on the following day, and by the third a continuous though thinly-occupied line was formed.

By the end of the first week it was held by 35,000 men. Small general reserve units were improvised by that time, including one platoon of five damaged tanks with limited mobility.

By the tenth day the division had improvised a full-strength, completely equipped motorcycle company utilizing men returning from furlough and convalescents. Several armored reconnaissance cars were turned over to this mobile reserve which could be moved to any danger spot along the *Rollbahn* [Ed: road designated as a main axis of motorized transportation] that ran parallel to and closely behind the front. This force was also versed in skiing and carried skis on the motorcycles in order to have cross-country mobility even though the snow was three feet deep in some places. This was a crack unit especially suited for local attacks and commanded by battle-tested officers.

The Luftwaffe signal battalion of VIII Air Corps at Novo-Dugino laid the necessary telephone lines and connected them with the air field switchboard. During the organization of the new front enemy attacks on the airfield and the adjacent sector to the north were repelled by alert units. In the central sector the enemy occupied several villages before the arrival of alert units. On the southern wing he occupied other villages and stood only a half to one mile from the highway which he interdicted with his mortars. At night enemy ski units infiltrated through the German lines, which initially were not continuous, and disrupted the supply of Ninth Army at several points between Vyazma and Rzhev. In view of the extreme cold and deep snow, the front line was almost exclusively a line of strong points based on villages. Although repeatedly under attack, the center of this line held from the outset.

Thus, the improvised front facing west served its initial purpose. Within a few days the whole sector threatened from the west was protected by alert units. Moreover, contact was established with the forces that fought in an arc around Rzhev to the north and with similarly improvised Fourth Army units in the south. However, the *Rollbahn* and the railroad were so close behind the front line that the continuous disruptions became unbearable. Furthermore, the slightest setback of the improvised units could result in the complete blocking of the traffic arteries by the enemy. This handicap could only be remedied by advancing the German outposts farther to the west. This involved a winter offensive in extreme cold and deep snow with improvised units which were without training in offensive operations. Yet, it had to be done. The operation could not be an offensive in the usual sense, let alone a blitzkrieg. The tactics to be used necessarily deviated from the conventional pattern and had to be especially suited to the peculiarities of the prevailing situation and the forces available.

3. *The Snail Offensive*   (Map 2)

At the beginning of February 1942, on the eighth day after the initial formation of the new front, the sector commanders were called to a meeting, informed of the necessity of an offensive, and indoctrinated in the combat methods to be used. The mere thought of starting an offensive with their motley units caused all commanders to raise serious objections which could be fully expressed by one single word: impossible. Only a detailed explanation of the tactics to be employed, for which the division commander coined the term "snail offensive," gradually dispelled the numerous objections which were perfectly valid from the conventional military standpoint.

First of all, it was pointed out to the commanders that time was not an important factor in this offensive. The speed of a snail would be sufficient. In selecting the place of attack they were to proceed like a snail which would move only to a place where it could find a worthwhile objective without incurring any danger. The method of advance was to resemble that of a snail slowly groping its way and immediately retracting its feelers or changing its direction whenever faced by an obstacle. Any setback must be avoided because it would discourage the weak German forces and tie them up for a long time just as a snail withdraws into its shell in a dangerous situation and does not dare continue on its way for quite a while. Nor were the commanders to forget the shell of the snail which affords safety and shelter in case of danger. Despite all precautions, however, the sector commanders had to keep in mind the rewarding objective at all times, exactly as a snail would do in the same situation.

This comparison served to illustrate the basic idea of the combat methods to be employed in the snail offensive. The practical application of this doctrine was subsequently explained at the site where the first offensive actions were to be launched. The objective of the snail offensive was to push back the Russians far enough to place the supply lines of Ninth Army beyond their reach. This meant that a line favorable for defense was to be reached which followed the edge of the vast wooded marshes. All villages in the fertile region to the east of it therefore had to be taken from the enemy. A secondary but important intention was to deprive the enemy of valuable shelter and sources of supply and to make these villages available to the German troops. This would be a hard blow to the enemy since there were only a few small, poor villages in the marshy forests, and the entire enemy force in the rear of Ninth Army was beginning to suffer from supply difficulties. After the Germans launched a successful panzer attack on Bely, the Russian force was practically surrounded by German units except for a narrow pathless strip across the front.

The final objective of the 6th Panzer Division was to roll back the enemy to a distance of ten to twenty miles from the *Rollbahn*, but this plan was at first not revealed to the commanders of the various sectors. The success of the initial operations was of paramount importance.

First of all, the central forces were ordered to eliminate the deep enemy wedge in the German lines. The enemy salient included three villages held by Russian security detachments. (See Map 2, Arrows ①.) There an initial victory should be easy to obtain. The attack was not to start until everything had been so well prepared that success could be expected with certainty. The three villages could be observed from the high German positions and dominated by cross fire from two sides. The enemy dispositions were under constant observation. The foremost village was held by the strongest enemy detachment, the two farther to the rear by smaller ones. A platoon of volunteers led by an experienced officer was to sneak up at night on each of the small villages, effect a penetration from the rear, make a surprise raid at dawn, and annihilate the enemy. Surprise was achieved, two villages were taken and the large one in front was cut off. Enemy attempts to break out during daytime were stopped by fire. At dusk the German forces in both villages were reinforced, the large village was surrounded, and the enemy force which attempted to break out under cover of darkness was captured. When all three villages were in German hands, they were immediately prepared for defense. Farther to the south another Russian strong point was taken by similar tactics. A strong covering force with heavy weapons remained in the old main line of resistance to stop any possible reverses. The main line of resistance was moved forward only after positions had been constructed in the frozen ground and supply and communication routes cleared of snow. As long as the enemy showed intentions of counterattacking, strong reserves were positioned behind the danger points and no further moves were initiated.

Similarly the initial operations in other sectors were adapted to local conditions and carried out at irregular intervals. The first week of the snail offensive resulted in the occupation of fourteen villages and the capture of numerous prisoners.

Losses on the German side were negligible. Most important was the confidence the German units gained in this combat method.

Gradually more complicated missions could be undertaken. However it remained essential to attack in the most effective manner and to reach the objective without becoming involved in a heavy engagement. Although the Russian forces in this sector were better trained and equipped, their supply of ammunition was limited and they were numerically too weak to organize a continuous line of defense. Their strong points were secured by outpost lines. The best method of overcoming these obstacles was to capture the villages where the outposts were located in order to isolate each main strong point until its encirclement was almost completed. Then the enemy troops usually abandoned their strong points voluntarily.

Bogdanovo, a village situated in dominating terrain on the southern wing, was one of the most important enemy strong points. From here the Russians frequently made thrusts into the adjacent sector to the south, penetrated to the *Rollbahn*, and stopped all traffic. In order to eliminate these inconvenient disruptions, the Fuehrer Escort Battalion, a crack SS unit which normally served as Hitler's personal bodyguard, was reinforced with heavy weapons and artillery and moved into the adjacent sector to take this enemy defense anchor by assault. After a short briefing and hasty preparations the battalion launched a frontal attack in the orthodox manner, forced the weak outposts to withdraw, and advanced almost to the edge of the main strong point. There the enemy, counterattacking from all sides and inflicting considerable losses, pushed back the battalion and encircled one company. The company was finally liberated under great difficulties, but the attack was not repeated because of the heavy casualties.

After this failure Ninth Army shifted the boundaries to include Bogdanovo in the 6th Panzer Division sector and ordered the division to capture it. Within a few days the snail offensive procedure scored another success by almost completely isolating the enemy strong point. When the divisional reserves attempted to close the ring, the Russians, though raked by heavy German fire, hastily evacuated the strong point in a daylight withdrawal. The village was immediately occupied and held against all later counterattacks.

In one month the snail offensive achieved the capture of eighty villages, and advanced the front line from five to eight miles. The principal effect, however, was to put the enemy on the defensive along the entire front, making thrusts in the direction of the *Rollbahn* and railroad out of the question. More and more battle-tested soldiers and reconditioned weapons had meanwhile been made available and supplied to the front. The number of tanks increased to eight, the artillery pieces to twelve. By then the operations of all units were well co-ordinated and the commanders had full confidence in the new combat tactics; thorough preparations and careful implementation of all instructions had prevented the slightest failure.

The subordinate commanders could now be granted much greater freedom for the continuation of the offensive. Division headquarters no longer interfered with details. Each sector was assigned a weekly phase line that was to be reached under optimum conditions. This line was not to be crossed without approval from division because safety considerations outweighed those of speed. Whenever the alert units ran into particular difficulties, they called upon divisional reserves which by now included a few tanks and dive bombers. All enemy attempts failed to halt the slow but steady advance of the improvised front. The snail offensive only paused in places where the enemy committed strong reserves; it started to move again immediately after these were transferred to another danger point. Since the enemy did not have sufficient forces and materiel to appear in strength in several places at the same time, he lost ground slowly but steadily. By the end of March 1942, two months after the start of the snail offensive, the Russians had been pushed back into the marshy forests and forced to relinquish more than two hundred villages.

This tactical, organizational, and logistical improvisation, a product of extreme emergency, had reached its intended objective. To go farther would have been impossible at this time because the two adjacent units had not joined the division in the offensive. The 6th Panzer Division units on the extreme ends of the sector had remained in their initial positions in order to prevent the opening of gaps in the flanks which would have permitted the enemy to infiltrate into the rear of the snail-offensive front. Ninth Army then widened the sector of 6th Panzer Division with orders to eliminate enemy interference in the adjacent areas by similar offensive action.

4. *The Scorpion Offensive*

Despite the successes obtained by the use of snail-offensive tactics in the central zone, the Germans holding the entire front facing west were still inferior to the opposing Russian forces which included some first-rate Guards units around Rzhev. It was the mission of the 6th Panzer Division to launch another offensive to push back the enemy from the only German highway and railroad line leading from Sychevka to Rzhev. (Map 3) The Russian outposts were located one to three miles from these essential supply routes and disrupted the traffic on many occasions.

The available forces and matériel were still inadequate for an offensive in the conventional manner. Once again it became necessary to improvise tactics. Only successive surprise attacks with limited objectives plus close co-ordination of all arms had any chance of success. Free choice of time and place for each intended thrust was another prerequisite since the issue would be in doubt if the enemy recognized the German intentions and took countermeasures. Whenever the element of surprise was lost, the objective had to be changed and the blow delivered at some distant vulnerable point. All this had to be achieved with a relatively weak striking force which was to be shifted to a different sector of the front immediately after each thrust. The tactics to be employed thus consisted of a well co-ordinated but flexible system of limited objective attacks. They could best be compared to a series of paralyzing stings a scorpion would inflict in a life-and-death struggle against a physically superior opponent.

Taken individually, the various lunges were not novel. A frontal break-through thrust in the center was followed by a double envelopment farther to the south. Only a few days later the same combat forces attacked through a deep forest to the north, accomplished their mission, and were immediately replaced by reserve units. Before the enemy had caught his breath, he was surprised by a deceptive thrust into his flank. Diagonal jabs at the northern and southern ends of the front consolidated the territorial gains achieved by the preceding operations. While the German forces suffered only slight losses, the enemy was prevented from seizing the initiative during the spring of 1942. He was dislodged from the favorable terrain he held and was forced to withdraw his forces approximately 12 miles along a 75-mile front. The German supply lines from Vyazma to Rzhev were finally secure, and a base of operations was acquired for the summer offensive which led to the annihilation of all Russian units holding out in the rear of Ninth Army.

5. *Cavalry Brigade Model in Operation* SEYDLITZ (Map 3)

The Russian elements that had broken through the German lines during the winter of 1941-42 and threatened the German supply lines during the spring, succeeded in gaining a foothold in the extensive, impassable, primeval forest swamps between Rzhev and Bely. Constantly receiving reinforcements of infantry, cavalry, and armored units, the Russians assembled a force of

60,000 men in the rear of Ninth Army and forced the Germans to fight on two fronts. They tied down strong forces and increasingly menaced the army rear. Russian supply arrived by a road leading via Poselok Nelidovo toward Bely.

In order to eliminate this danger and regain full freedom of action, General Model, commanding the Ninth Army, planned Operation SEYDLITZ, a concentric counterattack which started on 2 July 1942. During the first stage of the operation the Germans, in difficult forest fighting, dislodged the Soviet forces from their deeply-echeloned positions and hemmed them into a narrow area. A quick German thrust into the Obsha valley anticipated the apparent enemy intention of breaking through the newly-formed German switch position northeast of Bely. The Russians attacked simultaneously from the inside and the outside and attempted to escape through the breach thus made. The enemy units were split along the Obsha River and encircled in two pockets. All Russian attempts to break out were frustrated. Russian forces northeast of Bely directed relief attacks from the outside toward the pockets. These attacks were also repulsed. Strong tactical reserves which the enemy brought in by forced marches via Poselok Nelidovo arrived too late. After a battle lasting eleven days Operation SEYDLITZ ended with a complete German victory.

An improvised cavalry brigade, the formation of which General Model had ordered when Operation SEYDLITZ was still in the planning stage, played a major role in this success. Its organization was unique in many ways. Since most of the terrain was very swampy or covered with extensive marshy forests, the brigade was to be organized in such a manner that it would be able to fight in any terrain and under any weather conditions. It was even to be mobile in mud.

The first organizational problem was the procurement of men and equipment. Obviously only officers and enlisted men with combat experience in the East could be selected for such a specialized unit. Moreover they had to be trained cavalrymen. None but tough, healthy, brave men who were in no way pampered and who felt a close kinship with nature could be used. Replacements from the western theater or the zone of the interior were therefore out of the question because the troops from the West were softened by the easy ways of occupation life, and the recruits from the training camps at home lacked combat experience. Even though the latter had received a certain amount of specialized training for the eastern front, these recently inducted soldiers were incapable of enduring the physical hardships which the Russian theater imposed on the individual. There was not a commander in the field who was not aware that the difference between war in the East and war in the West was the difference between day and night.

General Model therefore decided to pull out the reconnaissance battalion from each of the eight divisions under his command and place them at the disposal of the newly appointed brigade commander. This was a very favorable solution for the brigade but hard on the infantry divisions, for the reconnaissance battalions were valuable combat units and were greatly missed by their parent divisions.

a. Organization and equipment of the brigade

The organization and equipment of the brigade was as follows:

(1)   A headquarters staff with one signal communication troop.

(2)   Three cavalry regiments, each consisting of one or two mounted troops and three to four bicycle troops, with a total of five troops per regiment. Within a few hours all mounted troops of the regiments could be assembled and a complete cavalry regiment formed for an emergency. Each troop had twelve sections and each section was equipped with two light machine guns. Thus each troop had twenty-four light machine guns and two heavies. In addition, officers and enlisted men were equipped with submachine guns when possible.

(3)   Each bicycle troop was issued two horse-drawn wagons which carried ammunition, baggage, and rations. Of course, these wagons were drawn by small native *Panje* horses because only they could master the terrain. The mounted troops had German military mounts. Mobility in mud was achieved because the *Panje* horses and wagons could pull through practically anywhere.

(4)   In addition, the brigade included an engineer company, a medical company, and one motorized and one horse-drawn supply column.

(5)   Tanks and antitank units were to assist the brigade whenever terrain conditions permitted. Each regiment had only six organic light infantry howitzers. Additional artillery support was also to be provided when necessary. The assistance of infantry and additional artillery units for flank protection was promised in case of a deep penetration or a break-through.

b. *Training and commitment of the brigade*

After about four to six weeks of combined arms training, the brigade was committed south of Olenino along the Luchesa River. A so-called *Rollbahn* led from Olenino southward which, although it was supposed to be a fairly good highway, was really no more than an unimproved country road. Short stretches of corduroy road covered particularly wet, swampy sections. Only the Luchesa valley was clear of woods to approximately one to three miles in width. Large, swampy forests extended on both sides of the valley with but a few clearings of varying sizes. Small, swampy creeks flowed through the woods. Maps and interrogation of local inhabitants provided the Germans with exact information on the terrain behind the enemy lines. Once the brigade had broken through the Russian positions at the edge of the woods, it would have to contend with swampy forests ten miles in depth where scarcely a path was to be found.

A panzer division was committed to the right of the brigade with the mission of attacking along the *Rollbahn* to the south. Since the Russians rightly expected the main effort of the attack along this axis of advance, the division was faced by a very difficult task. From aerial photographs and the interrogation of deserters it was known that strong enemy fortifications such as road blocks and fortified antitank positions were situated along the *Rollbahn*. The positions farther east and west from this road were not as strongly fortified but were secured by mine fields in which there were only a few gaps. The Russians thought it most improbable that a major attack could be launched east of the Luchesa River because the Germans would be unable to move tanks up to the line of departure through the swampy forests. They also felt certain that a tank attack across the open terrain, the Luchesa River, and through the mine fields would hardly be hazarded.

Approximately ten days before the attack the brigade moved up to the line of departure. Intensive reconnaissance of the intermediate terrain began immediately with the assistance of veteran tankers. Within a short time a complete picture of the enemy positions and the intervening terrain was available. From this picture it was obvious that, after the necessary preparations, an attack with armored support was definitely feasible.

For Operation SEYDLITZ the cavalry brigade was attached to its right neighbor, the panzer division which was to advance along the *Rollbahn*. The brigade was to thrust through the ten-mile-deep forest in one sweep and, if possible, cut the Russian supply line on the north-south highway if the main body of the panzer division was unable to make any progress. Six artillery batteries and one tank company with fourteen tanks were attached to the brigade for the execution of this mission.

The unit adjacent to the left, an infantry division, was not to jump off until the next day after the initial attack had been successful. For the first day the left flank would therefore be exposed. In the marshy forest terrain this was not a matter of particular concern because a small covering force would surely prove sufficient.

The first difficulties arose when the fourteen tanks had to be moved up to the line of departure through the swampy forests. Forty-eight hours before the beginning of the attack a company of engineers with power saws started to cut trees at intervals of about one yard along the edge of the forest so that the trees fell on open ground along a stretch leading through the assembly area. In a very short time and with relatively little effort a tank path was built which in effect was a corduroy road with about one-yard-wide gaps. Few branches had to be cut off the trees. For obvious reasons this road could only be used by a limited number of tanks and tracked vehicles.

A few hours after the engineers had gone to work the tanks started to move into their assembly area in daylight. This was possible because the wooded terrain afforded sufficient cover. The noise of the tanks was drowned by harassing fire and low-flying reconnaissance planes. All tanks arrived at their destination without incident. Experienced mine-clearing squads were assigned to each tank and ordered to ride on the tanks.

The attack started at 0300. During the artillery preparation the tanks started out together with the cavalry troops. Their movements were favored by a heavy fog which covered the river valley. They crossed most of the intervening terrain without encountering resistance. A ford across the Luchesa River which had been reconnoitered in advance was found to be adequate for the fourteen tanks. Enemy mine fields were immediately recognized by the experienced tankers and engineers and the lanes through the fields were found and widened. Suffering no losses, the tanks and cavalry suddenly rose in front of a completely surprised enemy. In one sweep the first and second lines were overrun and great confusion seized the Russians. The tanks had accomplished their mission. They could not penetrate any farther into the enemy-held forest without sufficient reconnaissance and additional preparation, and were therefore ordered to halt and stay in reserve. By then the cavalry had penetrated the enemy lines three to four miles.

The situation on the right was entirely different. Here the panzer division was to advance along the *Rollbahn.* The Russians were prepared for an attack. The German tanks ran into deeply echeloned antitank positions which were camouflaged with the usual Russian skill. The infantry also could not make headway and suffered heavy casualties in the forest fighting. The entire operation seemed in danger of bogging down.

At noon the brigade received orders to pivot toward the west with all available forces and to attack the *Rollbahn* from the east. One regiment turned to the right and thrust toward the *Rollbahn* through primeval forest swamps. At times the men sank in up to their knees. Direction had to be maintained by compass. The troops performed seemingly impossible feats and the surprise attack was a full success. By nightfall the regiment controlled a stretch of the *Rollbahn*, the pressure on the panzer division subsided, and the enemy was in an untenable position. The *Panje* supply wagons were able to move through the swamps and bring rations and ammunition to the completely exhausted troops.

On the following morning the continuation of the attack met hardly any resistance. On the other hand the physical requirements were extraordinarily high since the men had to traverse six miles of wooded swamps. Before noon the brigade emerged from the forest and a few hours later the first heavy equipment arrived. The terrain ahead extended over a wide area and Russian columns, single vehicles, and individuals could be seen moving about in wild disorder. It was obvious that the enemy command had lost control over its troops. The Russian defense lines had collapsed and the German divisions were advancing everywhere.

c. Conclusions

Even though Operation SEYDLITZ would probably have been successful without the cavalry brigade, it would have involved a much greater loss of men and equipment. During the eleven days of the operation 50,000 prisoners, 230 tanks, 760 artillery pieces, and thousands of small arms were captured. The situation of Ninth Army had been improved by the elimination of these Russian forces in its rear. The army rear area was safe except for partisan activities.

The composition of the brigade proved to be effective. The proper training for such a special mission requires from six to eight weeks with troops already experienced in Russian warfare. Before the attack the units must be in their jump-off positions for at least two weeks in order to become well-acquainted with terrain conditions through intensive reconnaissance. All intelligence and reconnaissance information must be carefully rechecked because the slightest inaccuracy can result in failure in that type of terrain.

Preliminary training in teamwork between armor and cavalry is of definite advantage. In an attack over this kind of terrain it may occasionally happen that the cavalry advances too fast. In that case the tanks must radio the cavalry to slow down because terrain difficulties prevent them from keeping up. Portable radio sets are not always reliable because of the density of the forest, and telephone communications therefore have to be used extensively. For that reason each·regiment must carry more than the customary quantity of wire.

If possible every officer and enlisted man should be equipped with a submachine gun.

Rations should be concentrated; the lighter they are, the better. The American combat ration (K ration) would be well suited, particularly since it is also protected against moisture.

It would be advantageous to equip troops with rubber boots and impregnated raincoats, camouflage jackets and windbreakers, because dew causes a high degree of moisture in the underbrush. Camouflage covers for steel helmets are essential and camouflage in general is of utmost importance.

The commissioned and noncommissioned officers must be versatile and able to make quick decisions and improvise. Every officer must be able to act independently and ready to assume responsibility. Detailed inquiries addressed to higher echelons cause delays and unfavorable developments which can usually be avoided. Leaders with good common sense and a portion of recklessness are best suited for such special assignments. The scholarly type of officer who relies chiefly on maps is completely out of place.

In general, it may be said that the composition and equipment of the cavalry brigade proved effective for the special mission of advancing and attacking through marshy forests and along muddy paths.

II. Some Improvisations Used During Operation ZITADELLE

1. The Crossing of Russian Mine Fields

In preparation for Operation ZITADELLE, the German pincer attack on Kursk during the summer of 1943, XI Infantry Corps made a thorough study of the problem of crossing the extensive mine fields on the east side of the Donets. The usual procedure of sending engineer detachments to clear narrow lanes for the advance of the infantry spearheads was not considered satisfactory since the terrain offered no cover and the enemy could inflict heavy casualties upon engineers and infantry by concentrating his fire on these lanes. Several improvised methods for overcoming this obstacle were therefore under consideration.

The identification of the mined area was the first prerequisite since the infantry had to know its exact location prior to the crossings. This was possible because the German-held west bank commanded the Russian positions on the other side of the river. Another prerequisite was that the infantry should be able to spot the location of individual mines at close range with the naked eye. In many places small mounds or depressions, dry grass, differences in the coloring of the ground, or some other external marks facilitated the spotting. The engineers had made a number of experiments in mine detecting. In the early days of the war, the infantry sometimes crossed narrow mine fields after individual engineers lay down beside the mines as human markers, taking great care not to set them off by pressure. Although neither engineers nor infantry troops suffered losses during these early experiments, the procedure was risky and could only be applied on a small scale. It was therefore of little consequence during the later stages of the war.

A second, more promising method that fulfilled expectations consisted of marking individual mines by placing small flags or other simple markers next to the mines. This was done by engineers or infantrymen who were trained in the recognition of mines. This procedure was applied repeatedly and showed better results than the first but its large-scale use presented difficulties. The third and best method was to thoroughly instruct all infantrymen in enemy mine-laying techniques and in spotting mines by using captured enemy mine fields as training grounds. This procedure required that all infantrymen be sent to rear areas in rotation and was therefore rather time-consuming.

These requirements could be met in the case of Operation ZITADELLE since the time of the attack had been twice postponed with an ensuing delay of several weeks. The divisions committed in the narrow attack zone had moved two thirds of their combat forces to the rear where the daily training schedule featured tanks passing over foxholes and the crossing of Russian-type mine fields. This training paid off since it helped the soldiers to overcome their fear of tanks and mines.

The beginning of the attack was so timed that the infantry would be able to detect the enemy mines without difficulty. All the mine fields were quickly crossed by spearheads which suffered practically no casualties. Only one battalion acted contrary to orders and attacked before daybreak, its commander being afraid that he might otherwise suffer heavy casualties from enemy fire while his men were crossing the extended open terrain in his zone. In the dark, this battalion ran into the previously uncovered mine fields and the two advance companies suffered approximately twenty casualties from mine explosions. When the battalion continued its advance by daylight it had no further losses.

After the first wave had passed through, the engineers rapidly cleared a number of lanes and marked them with colored tape so that the reserves and heavy weapons could follow. Again there were no mine casualties. Only when the supply units followed the infantry through the mine fields, were some of the men and horses blown up by the mines because they were careless or tried to bypass obstacles.

How safely anyone experienced in the detection of mines could move around in these mine fields was demonstrated during a conference on a completely mined hill, attended by about twenty unit commanders and specialists. No one had previously set foot on this hill but it was the only place which afforded a good view of the terrain. During the ascent of the hill each mine was clearly marked and no accidents occurred even though the mine field was crossed in various directions.

This improvised procedure of crossing mine fields became common practice because it avoided many casualties, resulted in quick capture of enemy positions, and was therefore very effective in the Russian theater.

2. A Flak Division Serves as Corps Artillery

In the plan for Operation ZITADELLE XI Infantry Corps was to cover the southern wing of the panzer corps that was to spearhead the attack. For this purpose corps was reinforced by two light motorized artillery battalions and by the fully reorganized 7th Flak Division. This Luftwaffe division, composed of three regiments with seventy-two 88-mm. and approximately 900 smaller antiaircraft guns, was to serve as a substitute for missing medium artillery.

According to Luftwaffe policy the subordination of Flak officers to Army unit commanders was prohibited. The corps artillery commander therefore depended on the voluntary cooperation of the Flak division commander. This led to repeated minor frictions but worked out quite well in general.

The division's first mission was to take part in the artillery preparation under the direction of the corps artillery commander. For this purpose the division was echeloned in depth and committed in three waves of one regiment each. The first echelon was in position in the main line of resistance and closely behind it; its mission was to place direct fire on enemy heavy weapons and pillboxes. In addition it had to form Flak assault detachments for antitank combat to give close support to the advancing infantry. Together with the corps artillery, the two other regiments were to shatter the first enemy line of defense and paralyze his infantry by delivering sustained concentrations. After that, elements of the first echelon, with the exception of the assault detachments, as well as the entire second echelon, were to support the advancing infantry. The third echelon was to take over the antiaircraft protection of the entire artillery area and was also to participate in counterbattery missions.

Enemy intelligence found out that the attack was to start on 5 July at dawn. The Russians laid down intensive harassing fire on the jump-off positions but this interference ceased as soon as the German artillery concentrations started. These were placed so well and the initial shock was so great that the first assault wave was able to cross the enemy mine fields, penetrate his main line of resistance without delay, and thrust a few hundred yards beyond it. Thousands of tracers fired by the numerous small Flak guns proved particularly effective. The Russians abandoned the trenches immediately and fled into their deep dugouts where the advancing infantry surprised them and had no difficulty in ferreting them out. But when the infantry reached the two-to three-mile-deep zone of battle positions prepared during the preceding months, they had to make extensive use of hand grenades in order to mop up the maze of deeply dug-in trenches and bunkers, some of which were a dozen or more feet deep. At the same time artillery and Flak fired counterbattery on enemy heavy weapons which resumed fire from rear positions, on reserves infiltrating through trenches, and on medium artillery. The third echelon of the antiaircraft division was fully occupied with defense against enemy bombers which attacked the corps area incessantly. During the first two hours they downed more than twenty enemy planes.

Within eight hours the German infantry penetrated the enemy fortification system in its entire depth and reached the railroad embankment parallel to the Donets. Suddenly a Russian counterattack supported by forty tanks threw back the German covering force from the woods on the south flank and hit the right wing division which was echeloned in depth. But the defensive fire of the divisional artillery and a concentration of all medium antiaircraft batteries stopped the enemy counterattack at the edge of the forest. Then the medium Flak was directed against tank concentrations, which had been recognized in the underbrush, and dispersed them. Repeated enemy attempts to resume the attack from this area failed without exception. Flank protection was soon restored and the threat eliminated.

On the second day of the operation, the high ground ahead was captured under the protection of Flak artillery fire; all counterthrusts were repelled. On the morning of the third day the enemy attempted to recover lost ground and counterattacked with two heavy tank brigades and motorized infantry units. The tanks overran the battle line of the German infantry and penetrated deeply, but the motorized infantry which followed was repelled. The enemy tank break-through hit the corps center behind which, however, several Flak assault detachments and numerous medium antitank guns were sited in a mutually-supporting formation. The enemy ran into this dense network of antitank defenses as well as a flank attack by thirty-two assault guns and was completely annihilated. The last enemy tank which had penetrated to a divisional command post was surprised by an assault detachment carrying gasoline cans and was set on fire. Sixty-four enemy tanks had begun the counterattack and two hours later sixty-four black columns of smoke gave proof of their destruction. Discouraged by his failure, the enemy made no further attempts at an armored break-through at any point of the corps sector even though he had plenty of additional armored units available. The improvised commitment of the antiaircraft division contributed decisively to this defensive success and the formation of Flak assault detachments proved highly effective in the destruction of Russian armor.

Chapter 2

The Defensive

I. Improvised Hedgehog Defenses

From the very first days of the campaign, the vastness of European Russia and the peculiarities of Russian warfare led to the repeated isolation of individual units and combat teams. All-around defenses and security measures were the only possible remedy. Far from being stressed, these defense tactics were frequently not even mentioned in the field service regulations. The field forces improvised them and designated them very appropriately as "hedgehog defenses." As time went on these tactics were applied more and more frequently and adopted by larger units. Their use was not confined to defense. During offensive actions advance detachments had to build hedgehog defenses as protection against enemy surprise attacks by night. For instance, during their advance through a swampy forest region in Lithuania where strong, dispersed enemy forces were reassembling, combat teams of 6th Panzer Division formed the first hedgehog positions during the initial week of the Russian campaign. Several hay barns in a major clearing were selected as the location for the divisional command post. Covered by thick underbrush, the tanks were placed in a wide circle around the barns with their guns ready to fire at the edge of the woods. In front of the tanks was an outer ring of infantry in foxholes and ditches and behind embankments which enabled the tanks to fire over their heads. Security patrols and outposts formed an outer cordon. The Russians recognized the strength of these protective measures and did not dare carry out the surprise attack they had planned. They resigned themselves to harassing the hedgehog area with tank and machine gun fire and a few rounds of artillery shells.

The hedgehog defense provided the troops with security and rest and thus passed its first major test. Before long these precautions became a routine security and defense measure for armored spearheads. The first large-scale employment of this measure occurred during the thrust toward Vyazma in October 1941 when an entire panzer division with 260 tanks spent the first night of the attack in an elaborate system of hedgehog positions in the woods. (Map 1) Forming the spearhead of a powerful wedge, the division had penetrated the enemy lines to a depth of twenty miles. In its rear and on its flanks defeated enemy divisions were withdrawing under cover of darkness. A retreating enemy corps staff sought refuge in a small isolated village in the forest which was occupied by the German divisional staff. Enemy troop units were around the entire system of tank hedgehogs. As long as the German tanks were on their own, the intermittent firing of flares and machine guns indicated their great uneasiness. This changed with the arrival of the armored infantry which followed the tanks. When the divisional artillery and engineers arrived and were also integrated into the hedgehog defense system, a restful night was had by all. Early next morning the Russians departed very quietly because they were unable to find any rest in the immediate vicinity of the German division.

II. Defensive Improvisations in Extreme Cold

During the last days of 1941, the 6th Panzer Division was outmaneuvered by superior Russian forces and dislodged from a chain of villages which surrounded a large forest region. The division was faced with two alternatives: It could either withdraw a certain distance to another group of communities and be enveloped and split up, or it could establish defense positions in front of or between these indefensible villages in a temperature of −49° F. without adequate shelter which would mean certain death from exposure. During the engagements of the last few days, most of which had of necessity taken place in open terrain, the daily casualties from frostbite had increased at an alarming rate. By 3 January 1942 the number of moderate and severe frost bite casualties had risen to 800 per day. At that rate the division would soon have ceased to exist. The immediate construction of shelters and bunkers, with whatever heating facilities could be installed, was mandatory. But these defensive positions could not be built because only one corps and two divisional engineer battalions with 40 to 60 men each and very little equipment were available. On the other hand a large quantity of explosives had recently arrived at division. In view of the critical situation, the engineer battalion commanders were ordered to disregard the frost and to blast enough craters into the solidly frozen ground along the tentative defense line to provide shelter for all combat units including the reserves. These craters were to be echeloned in width and depth and were to hold three to five men each. The engineers were also to mine certain areas and build tank obstacles in three places. The reserves and service troops were ordered to pack down paths between the craters and to the rear. They were to use readily available lumber to cover the craters.

The blasting along the entire line started early next morning. The noise of the 10,000-pound explosive charges somehow gave the impression of a heavy barrage. Fountains of earth rose all around and dense smoke filled the air. The enemy watched with surprise, could not understand what was happening, and remained quiet. The blasting was over by noon and by nightfall the craters were covered and occupied by the combat elements. Soon afterward smoke rose from the craters where the crews kept warm at open fires. The craters formed an uninterrupted line of positions in front of which outposts were established. A maze of abatis lay in front of these, guns were emplaced along the thoroughfares behind the tank obstacles, and the entire front line was ready for defense within twelve hours after the first detonation. This position withstood all enemy attacks and was not abandoned until ten days later, in milder weather, when the adjacent units on both wings were forced to withdraw after enemy tanks had penetrated their lines.

The engineers who prepared the positions in the fiercest cold and suffered 40 percent frostbite casualties saved the combat units and restored the situation by their sacrifice. The very next day the casualties from frostbite dropped from 800 to 4 cases and thus practically ceased.

This improvisation was introduced at a time when 6th Panzer Division had lost all its tanks during the preceding withdrawal. Before blasting the positions, fighting had centered upon the possession of villages which alone could offer shelter from the extreme cold. Groups of villages had formed natural phase lines for both the attacker and the defender who had been forced to ignore all other tactical considerations. Whenever the Russians failed to capture a village by day, they withdrew to the last friendly village for the night. Not even the best-equipped Siberian troops attempted to continue an attack on a village after dusk. Blasting positions in open terrain was therefore an innovation that served the double purpose of stabilizing the front and maintaining the combat efficiency of the remnants of the division.

On another occasion the blasting of ice proved much less effective. In order to prevent the enemy from making an enveloping thrust across Lake Pskov on the Russian-Estonian border during the winter of 1943–44, Army Group North blasted a ten-foot-wide, several-mile-long canal into the ice north of the isle of Salita. At that time the ice was so thick that it could carry medium guns and prime movers. But here, as in other instances, it became apparent that the blasting of ice created no permanent obstacle because the water froze immediately in the extreme cold and shortly afterward the ice was again capable of carrying heavy loads. In extremely low temperatures all attempts to stop enemy advances by blasting frozen bodies of water were doomed to fail.

Almost a year later, toward the end of 1944, the Germans devised another improvisation to prevent the Russians from crossing a frozen body of water. By late autumn the Russians had driven a wedge into the German front near Memel [Ed: now Klaipeda] and had reached the Kurisches Haff. (Map 4) The Germans intended to prevent the landing of enemy forces on the west side of the Haff. A large-scale landing was not expected because the prerequisites for such an undertaking did not exist, but it seemed quite likely that the enemy would attempt to land sabotage or raiding parties, spies, agents, or commandos along the coast under cover of darkness. The coastal defenses composed of service units, volunteer organizations, and Volkssturm [Ed: Peoples' militia assembled during the last years of the war] supported by weak reserve elements from Koenigsberg [Ed: now Kaliningrad] were thought to be sufficient to thwart any such operation.

It was a known fact that the Haff froze over in winter and that the ice cover would carry men and vehicles. This might encourage enemy attempts to envelop the exposed German wing, cut off the only supply route to Memel, or undertake some other major operation. For that reason plans were drawn up to block the Kurisches Haff in its entire width of ten miles.

In the late fall of 1944 a number of wooden bunkers with heating facilities were constructed for this purpose. They were approximately five feet high and could hold a crew of three to five men and their weapons. The bunkers were placed on rafts with sled runners in order to give them mobility on ice and simultaneously to protect them from sinking into the water in case the ice suddenly broke. This possibility had to be taken into account because of the sudden changes in temperature which occur in this area. By the end of December 1944 the first groups of bunkers were moved onto the freezing Haff, the edges of which were by then sufficiently strong to carry them. The bunker positions were spread over the ice as the freezing process progressed. Approximately 150 bunkers were laid out in two parallel lines in checkerboard formation, giving each other fire support. The bunkers were reinforced with blocks of ice on the outside and camouflaged with snow. A continuous line of entanglements with alarm signals was to prevent the enemy from infiltrating between the bunkers. Reserves were held in readiness behind both lines of bunkers. Ice boats and motor sleighs needed by the reserves to give them mobility did not arrive in time and the plans for organizing a combined ice-boat and motor-sleigh brigade had to be abandoned. Artillery support was provided from both shores.

Since the Russians lacked fast means of transportation on ice, they could only have advanced on foot over the long distances of the Haff. This was probably the reason why they failed to attack during the winter and this improvised position was therefore never put to the test.

III. A Moving Pocket Regains the German Lines

In some instances German divisions were left behind the Russian advance and were forced to fight their way back to the west. For example during the large-scale Russian offensive in the winter of 1942, the 320th Infantry Division, which had held a sector on the Don front with two Italian divisions at its sides, suddenly found itself behind the enemy lines because of the rapid disintegration of the allied units. The division commander decided to fight his way back to the German lines. On the way all the divisional motor vehicles ran out of gasoline and had to be destroyed. The horse-drawn batteries and trains also lost a great number of horses in battle and from exhaustion. Altogether, the fighting power and mobility of the division was greatly impaired. If it was not to resign itself to its fate, it had to resort to improvisations. What was needed either had to be wrested from the enemy or taken from the land. In this manner the division procured hundreds of small draft horses for the light vehicles. The medium artillery was drawn by oxen. Cows and oxen were used as draft animals for the transportation of radio and signal equipment. Even the division commander decided to use such a team as a sure means of transportation. The loss of many weapons such as machine guns, antitank guns, and artillery pieces could only be offset by weapons captured from weak enemy detachments on occasional raids. The ammunition needed for the use of captured weapons was also taken from the enemy and the same methods were applied in obtaining rations. Small radio sets and other sensitive equipment had to be carried on litters. Infantrymen mounted on *Panje* horses were charged with reconnaissance and security. The difficult retreat of the division took several weeks and was an uninterrupted series of marches, combat actions, and improvisations. As the division approached Kharkov, it suddenly made radio contact and asked the German units in the city for assistance in its attempt to break through to the German lines. A strong armored thrust from inside the city was co-ordinated with a simultaneous attack by the division. The enemy lines were pierced at the point designated by the division and it was able to rejoin the German lines. Its appearance hardly resembled that of a German unit. A strange conglomeration of weapons, equipment, vehicles, and litters, small and large shaggy horses, oxen and cows, accompanied by soldiers in a variety of winter clothing created the impression of a traveling circus on parade. And yet it was a battle-tested unit with excellent morale that had courageously fought its way through enemy territory, had returned to its own lines, and was to be considered a precious addition to the corps strength. By the following day the division once again stood shoulder to shoulder with the other corps units and held a sector facing east. Its strong will to survive and skillful improvisations enabled the division to regain its freedom.

IV. Zone Defense Tactics

During the last years of the war, Russian break-throughs were accomplished by the same methods that had been employed so successfully by the same enemy in World War I. These methods had little in common with customary tactical doctrines but were based on great superiority of manpower and matériel. After weeks of logistical build-up and moving up the enormous quantities of ammunition needed, the German front was breached after several hours of concentrated fire. This was followed by the break-through of massed infantry forces and deep thrusts of armored units in order to gain freedom of maneuver. The system was absolutely foolproof so long as the opponent did not interfere with the sequence of events. An essential prerequisite was that the defender would rigidly hold that sector of the front, which was to be attacked, until he received the deadly blow. In the East the Germans complied with this prerequisite since their forces had strict orders not to relinquish one inch of ground voluntarily. These defense tactics were enforced almost without exception until the end of the war. Being aware of the army's numerical inferiority and its loss of combat efficiency caused by heavy casualties, Hitler perhaps doubted its capability of conducting a flexible active defense and therefore ordered all army units to cling rigidly to prepared positions. But such tactics could never prevent an enemy break-through, let alone lead to victory. Despite the fact that Russian casualties were relatively heavier than those suffered by the Germans and the fighting qualities of the Russian soldiers vastly inferior to those of their opponents, the always-present crucial problem was to make up for the Russian superiority in men and matériel. Aside from their greater fighting capabilities the Germans had no other means of offsetting their inferiority than by employing more flexible and superior tactics. If the military leaders lost their faith in the superiority of the German armed forces in these two fields, or if shortages of matériel became so acute that these advantages could not be exploited, then a favorable outcome of this war was no more to be expected than in World War I. It was the responsibility of the Supreme Commander, Adolf Hitler, to recognize this fact and draw the necessary conclusions. Until that time it was the duty of the commanders in the field to do their utmost to prevent a collapse of the front lines. The greatest imminent threats to the fighting front were the Russian massed attacks with subsequent break-throughs. Since adequate reserves for successful defense were rarely available, it became all the more necessary to prevent the annihilation of the front-line units by Russian fire concentrations, bombing attacks, and massed armored thrusts in order to preserve their combat efficiency.

An improvisation devised for this purpose was the zone defense tactics introduced toward the end of the war. It was derived from an analysis of the reasons for the success of most enemy break-throughs. The principal factors to be considered were the following:

  a. The annihilation of front-line troops by mass concentration on points along the main line of resistance;

  b. The neutralization or destruction of the German artillery by heavy counterbattery fire and continuous air attacks;

  c. The elimination of command staffs by air attacks and surprise fire on command posts up to army level;

  d. The harassing of reserves by artillery fire and air attacks on their assembly areas;

  e. The disruption of the routes of communication to the front which delayed movements of reserves and cut off supply;

  f. The massed armored thrusts in depth which enabled the Russians to obtain freedom of maneuver.

For obvious reasons the task of the defender was to neutralize these enemy tactics or at least to reduce them to tolerable proportions. One of the panzer armies in the eastern theater devised the following defense measures and employed them successfully:

a. There were two ways of preventing the annihilation of the frontline troops: either by constructing bombproof and shellproof positions or by withdrawing the forward units in time to evade the devastating barrages. Since the construction of shellproof positions required an expenditure of time and materials beyond the German capabilities, the adoption of evasive tactics was the only solution. Such evasive tactics had already been employed during the last stage of World War I. The forward positions were evacuated shortly before an imminent attack and the defending troops moved far enough to the rear into a new and even stronger line to force the enemy to regroup his forces, always a time-consuming maneuver. The difficulties encountered by the enemy before he was able to resume the attack were to be enhanced by demolitions in the intermediate terrain. These evasive tactics were tried out in 1918 in the West when the German combat forces withdrew to the Hindenburg Position and in the South on the Italian front along the Piave River. The loss of some ground which was involved in the application of these tactics was a well-considered sacrifice. But to achieve a permanent gain was possible only if the new positions could be held without fail. Another method of evading fire concentrations and a subsequent break-through was the adoption of elastic defense tactics in a deeply echeloned system of machine gun strong points which, however, often lacked the necessary resiliency to stop a major enemy attack.

A method frequently applied by the Germans as another form of evasion can best be compared with saber-fencing tactics. A cut is warded off by sudden retirement with appropriate guard, followed by an immediate counterthrust which will permit the fencer to regain his former position. Like the fencer, the forces holding the threatened sector of the front executed a surprise withdrawal at the last moment. They moved far enough to the rear so that the blow would miss them, the pursuing enemy could be repelled, and the initial position could be regained by a counterthrust. In order to satisfy these requirements, the terrain in which the pursuing enemy was to be intercepted had to be well chosen and systematically prepared in order that the withdrawing forces could resume the defense within a few hours. It was therefore neither possible nor essential to withdraw the front-line units so far to the rear that they were out of reach of enemy guns. Past experience indicated that the enemy fired his concentrations only on the main line of resistance and on strong points in the zone of resistance. For this reason it was absolutely necessary to evacuate this zone. Depending on the terrain and local fortifications, it was usually quite sufficient to withdraw the most forward troops 900 to 2,200 yards. Here was the forward edge of the battle position, a well-camouflaged organized system of defense that took advantage of all favorable terrain features. Numerous strong points and sizable local reserves were distributed throughout the position which extended back to the artillery emplacements and even beyond. In a camouflaged area behind the artillery were the general reserves of corps and army. By following this procedure, targets were so well dispersed that fire from as many as a thousand guns directed at so large an area could cause only local damage but could never wipe out entire units.

b. If the German artillery was to avoid neutralization and escape destruction it had to switch to alternate emplacements in the battle position at the decisive moment. In addition the artillery also had to use alternate observation posts. These alternate positions had to be prepared well in advance, provided with ammunition, and equipped with a smoothly functioning wire and radio communication system. Additional battery positions and observation posts had to be reconnoitered and organized in depth so that they would be ready for immediate occupancy and utilization in case of emergency. This was to guarantee continuous support for the infantry even in the event of a reverse since only the flexible employment of artillery units which were always intact and ready to strike promised a successful defense. Furthermore, each battery had to establish two or three additional alternate positions and one or two dummy positions and had to fire from them with at least one registration gun in order to determine firing data for every emplacement. Altogether between five and eight positions had to be prepared by each battery. The Russian build-up allowed sufficient time for such extensive preliminary work and the Germans could therefore devote several weeks to these preparations.

c. All necessary precautions had to be taken to protect the command staffs and their communication system from destruction by artillery preparations and the ensuing general attack. For that reason no command staff from battalion up to army was permitted to stay at the command post it occupied before the start of the enemy attack. Each staff had to prepare a well-camouflaged, shellproof command post away from inhabited communities and was required to install a telephone switchboard in a separate bunker. Communications with the command post had to be assured by wire, radio, visual signals, dispatch riders, or runners, and in an emergency by a combination of these various means of communication. Telephone wires had to be laid in such manner that they could not easily be cut by fire or tracked vehicles; wherever possible they were laid along ditches and swampy depressions or strung on trees. Radio trucks had to be dug into the ground in inconspicuous places, protected against fragments, and well camouflaged before the attack started. Then strict radio silence had to be enforced.

d. Before the general attack, all reserves had to leave their billeting areas and move into the battle-position quarters which had to be well camouflaged, outside inhabited communities, and ready for immediate use. Telephone, radio, and other communication media had to be readily available.

e. The routes of communication to the front were of vital importance and therefore had to be kept open under all circumstances. Bottlenecks had to be avoided, defective stretches of road made serviceable even in inclement weather, and strict traffic control imposed for two-way traffic. Alternate bridges had to be built in suitable places away from the existing ones and provided with approach roads. At least two alternate routes had to be determined through each community so that convoys could detour narrow streets whenever there was danger of air attacks.

f. One of the major problems was to intercept massed armored attacks and prevent break-throughs. This involved extensive countermeasures which could only gradually be enforced and slowly integrated into the defense system.

First of all the terrain particularly suited for an armored break-through was mined to a quite unusual extent. Selecting such areas and mining them with due consideration for Russian tactical doctrine presented little difficulty to an experienced panzer expert. The numerous mine fields

were to be laid in depth and width in a checkerboard pattern
in such a manner that the German armored units could detour them on the basis of information received. All signs
designating mine fields were removed prior to the enemy
attack. No mines were laid in front of the German main
line of resistance because the enemy could have removed
them and used them for his own purposes before the start
of the attack. The main battle position was mined in
depth up to fifteen miles to the rear. Prior to the major
offensive in the area east of Lvov during the summer of
1944, the sector where the main attack thrust was expected was mined with 160,000 antipersonnel and 200,000
antitank mines within the zone defense. This was the first
time that the Germans applied zone defense tactics of the
type described in this study.

The most forward divisional antitank guns had to take up
positions approximately one mile behind the main line of
resistance. The bulk of the artillery and numerous medium
antitank and antiaircraft guns were to form centers of gravity behind the forward guns up to twelve miles in depth. In
addition, all roads suitable for sudden armored thrusts
in depth were blocked by tank obstacles, captured im-
mobile antitank guns, and antiaircraft guns emplaced at
all important points up to a depth of twenty-five miles.
In case of critical developments numerous self-propelled
antitank guns were to reinforce the defense. To camouflage these guns, tank ditches had to be dug and approach
roads built in suitable terrain.

The army reserves had to be sufficiently strong to support
the front and stop the enemy in case he suddenly shifted
his main effort and turned his tanks to an adjacent sector
which had not been prepared according to zone defense
principles. For instance, during the battle near Lvov the
army commander held in reserve five strong panzer divisions which he had withdrawn from sectors that were not
in immediate danger. Two of them were to support the
front in the center of gravity and the three strongest
were to be instantly committed to stop any armored thrust
elsewhere in case the enemy shifted his point of main effort. The two divisions assigned to the center of gravity
were expected to be able to lend them assistance in due
course. The reserves formed mobile battle groups and
equipped them with many antitank and assault guns in

order to enable them to give immediate support to front-line sectors threatened by sudden disintegration. In most cases these battle groups consisted of reconnaissance or . motorcycle battalions reinforced by antitank and assault gun battalions which were held in instant readiness and formed advance detachments of their respective divisions.

The task of indoctrinating the unit commanders in all the essential zone defense measures was far from easy. After detailed briefings, map exercises, and tactical walks, they not only grasped the idea but became thoroughly convinced of the expediency and feasibility of the plan and lent their enthusiastic support to its execution. Discussions and training exercises continued down the line to the smallest units.

The next step was to put these measures to their practical test and examine them in the light of experience. Starting with individual arms, these tests were later extended to larger units. Finally, zone defense tactics were adopted and enforced by entire divisions and corps. The tremendous effort entailed in these preparations was to pay high dividends.

The fencer derives an advantage from cutting into his opponent's sequence when the latter intends to strike because the attacker usually exposes himself on that occasion. This intercepting blow was also included in the zone defense tactics. Since the enemy moved his forces close to his most advanced positions and massed them there before jumping off to attack, he exposed himself to concentrated surprise fire from all artillery pieces and rocket launchers. Two basic loads of every type of ammunition had been set aside for just that purpose.

The most difficult and critical problem was to determine the correct time for withdrawing to the battle position. If too late a moment was chosen, the safety measures against the annihilation of the combat forces by an enemy barrage would have remained ineffective. The front-line units and intermediate commands alone were unable to gather sufficient positive clues regarding the hostile intentions to enable the higher echelons to draw the correct conclusions as to when the enemy attack would begin. This can be easily understood since their observation of enemy activities was restricted to the most advanced areas of the front. But well-organized combat intelligence and constant air observation, co-ordinated by the army commander in person, gathered so much information on enemy preparations and covered his rear areas so completely that the H Hour for the attack could be determined with a high degree of accuracy. The most reliable information was secured by radio interception. As much as 70 percent of all reliable information was obtained from this source.

The improvised defense system was first applied in the summer of 1944 in the battle of Lvov and for the second time in January 1945 during the second battle for East Prussia. In both instances the Russians attacked at precisely the point and in exactly the manner expected by the army commander who devised this zone defense system. H Hour for the enemy attack in East Prussia was determined to the exact day and hour. In the battle near Lvov, however, the enemy started his offensive two days later than expected. Interrogation of prisoners confirmed that the attack was postponed by two days at the last moment. As a result the evasive maneuver had to be repeated on three successive nights. On the first day the Russians either did not notice the withdrawal because German rear guards left in the forward positions simulated the weak routine harassing fire or they lacked time to react to this-sudden change. On the second day they attacked several evacuated positions with combat teams up to regimental strength and pushed back the rear guards.

Even this turn of events was foreseen in the original plan. Strong counterthrusts supported by massed artillery fire from the regular firing positions sealed off the enemy penetrations and at dusk the former main line of resistance was once again occupied by the infantry. As expected, the enemy resumed his attacks during the night to find out whether the Germans would continue to occupy the positions. When these night attacks had been repelled everywhere and the Russians had convinced themselves that the positions were held by their full complements, the fighting broke off and the front calmed down. After midnight the positions were evacuated for the third time and, when the enemy fire concentration was unleashed at dawn, it hit empty positions. The units that had moved into the battle position suffered hardly any losses and, supported by assault guns and one battalion of Royal Tiger tanks, they were able to drive back nearly all Russian forces which had advanced beyond the empty positions. The artillery preserved its entire fire power because the shelling and air bombardment hit the empty battery positions which assumed the role of dummies. Not a single gun, not a single command post was hit. The telephone communications from army down to regiment suffered no disruption. But the former positions that had been evacuated were in poor shape. The towns were badly damaged by air attacks, and the debris of bombed buildings blocked the main roads in several villages. Nevertheless, the traffic continued to move along the previously designated alternate routes and was stopped only intermittently whenever the enemy air force scored direct hits on convoys.

The reserves were left untouched by the air attacks directed against them since they had moved to locations that were unknown to the enemy. The advancing Russian infantry was hit by the defensive fire of an artillery and rocket launcher brigade which was fully intact and well supplied with ammunition. When the enemy infantry attempted to disperse and take cover it walked straight into the mine fields which had been laid behind the German main line of resistance. This took the momentum out of the attack and prevented the Russian infantry from concentrating its effort in one direction. The advance slowed down and became hesitant. Practically all territorial gains had to be abandoned by the Russians when the German troops that had evaded the destructive effect of the initial barrage started to counterattack later during the day. The distress signals sent out by the Russian infantry brought their armor to the scene. Like a cataract released by the sudden opening of a dam, the massed armor poured across the Seret River into the historic battle ground of Yaroslavichi where exactly thirty years before, during the summer of 1914, Austro-Hungarian and Russian cavalry divisions had clashed head on in the last major cavalry charge in history.

History repeated itself. Once again the Russians had numerical superiority and once again the battle ended in a draw. In 1914 the defender achieved this result by the use of new machine gun and artillery tactics whereas in 1944 he introduced zone defense tactics to overcome his inferiority. On the very first day of the armored attack, the enemy lost eighty-five tanks in the mine fields. The number of tanks lost increased rapidly when the armored thrust came within reach of the antitank guns and was brought to a halt. The losses assumed truly disastrous proportions when the German panzer divisions proceeded to counterattack.

In 1914 as in 1944 the battles for Lvov were not decided by the cavalry charge or the armored thrust near Yaroslavichi but by a major Russian break-through north of Lvov in the adjacent army sector to which the enemy shifted his main effort. Unfortunately for the Germans in 1944, the SS panzer corps with the three strongest panzer divisions had previously been transferred to the Western Front because the Allies had meanwhile landed in France. For this reason sufficient forces were no longer available to stop the Russian armored drive in the new area of penetration.

V. Improvised Fortresses

By 1944, after the Germans had suffered a succession of defeats, Hitler frequently tried to reverse the tide by the arbitrary designation of fortresses. In the face of an imminent enemy attack, many towns suddenly became improvised fortresses and had to suffer encirclement and siege as if they were well-equipped strongholds that had been systematically constructed and provisioned over a number of years. A commander was appointed for each fortress, given absolute powers, and put under a special oath. He thereby received authority of life and death over all persons within his jurisdiction and could employ them as he saw fit, even though most of them were merely passing through his territory. These men and their equipment were frequently the only resources at the disposal of the commander who actually was forced to pick them off the streets.

Thus, the city of Kolberg was declared a fortress early in March 1945 when the battle for Pomerania was in full swing. The small city was overcrowded with wounded, the railroad station filled with hospital trains. Columns of refugee carts blocked the roads and enemy tanks were only twenty-five miles off. Precisely at that moment the newly appointed fortress commander who was entirely unfamiliar with the situation was flown in by plane. He was not acquainted with the duties of a fortress commander and had to be briefed in detail. The fortress was absolutely defenseless. Hitler's attention was called to this fact, but he nevertheless decided that Kolberg must be held as a fortress under all circumstances. In his reply Hitler stated that the Spandau depot would receive instructions to immediately dispatch twelve new antitank guns to Kolberg by rail. This was at a time when the single-track railroad line to Kolberg was completely blocked and enemy tanks were expected to appear in the immediate vicinity of the city within a few hours. Obviously, the antitank guns never arrived. The commander was forced to pick his defense force and weapons from the streets. Indiscriminately everybody and everything moving through the city was stopped, whether they were Luftwaffe, naval personnel, damaged tanks, antiaircraft, antitank, or artillery guns, and integrated into the fortress defenses.

It was difficult to imagine why Hitler decided that this former small coastal fort should be defended, unless for historical reasons. In modern times, however, the events that occurred in Napoleon's day could not possibly be repeated. However, the enemy seemed to be impressed by the glorious past of the city because his approach was slow and hesitant. The first Russian attack was delayed for two days, but the defensive tactics employed by the Germans soon revealed their weakness and after only a few days the enemy captured the city. Most of the entirely improvised garrison was rescued by the Navy.

The location of some of the fortresses was so unfavorable that their defense seemed hopeless from the outset. Despite all remonstrances, even these places had to be held at all cost. For instance, Brody, a small town in eastern Galicia completely surrounded by woods, was located in a valley without observation facilities. Dominated by a nearby plateau in enemy hands, the town was under complete enemy observation and at the mercy of his artillery. At one point the woods even reached up to the edge of the town. Because of the lack of space, there was not even a suitable area for the artillery emplacements in case of a siege. In order to avoid an imminent disaster, the army commander circumvented Hitler's orders and adopted tactics that prevented a siege of the town.

The situation at Ternopol was similar; there the garrison held out bravely for one month only to succumb for lack of rations and ammunition after an attempt to break the siege had bogged down in the mud.

By the end of January 1945 one of the German panzer armies had three of its best divisions in Fortress Koenigsberg, two in Fortress Memel, and only the two weakest at its disposal for operations in the field. At this decisive time an entire army group with the best available troops was hemmed in in Kurland and eliminated from participation in the defense of the German homeland because it had strict orders to hold out in place.

These tactics were championed by Hitler in person and enforced with all the authoritative powers at his disposal. In the end they obstructed all operational freedom and devoured the very substance of the German Army until there was no army left.

But the picture was entirely different whenever the encircled forces broke out and remained intact. In February 1943 Kharkov was surrounded by enemy armies and ordered to hold out in a hopeless situation. In his last telephone message the corps commander called attention to the seriousness of the situation and stated emphatically that the only choice was between losing the city alone or losing the city with all the troops in it. The reply was that "Kharkov must be held to the last man." On the following morning a second order came through by teletype stating that "Kharkov must be held to the last man but the defenders must not allow themselves to be encircled." On the strength of this ambiguous order, the second part of which precluded the first, the encircled corps took immediate steps for a breakout to the rear without the knowledge or approval of army. After two days of hard fighting, which ended with the loss of several hundred motor vehicles, this corps rejoined the German lines. The decision proved to be correct for, together with some divisions detrained in the Poltava area under its protection, the corps was able to launch a counterattack only one month later, recapture Kharkov and Belgorod, and reach the upper Donets.

This example demonstrates very convincingly that it is not of decisive importance to hold a town at all cost but rather to have some forces available for further operations.

VI. Defensive Improvisations in East Prussia

As the danger of an invasion of eastern Germany loomed toward the end of 1944, tens of thousands of civilians were mobilized to construct a number of continuous defense lines in East Prussia. Everywhere people could be seen digging trenches and defense positions. Altogether twelve main defense lines and switch positions were constructed, many of which were well equipped. Perhaps their most outstanding feature was the construction of improvised machine gun emplacements which were very practical and consisted of two large concrete pipes. One pipe stood upright in the ground and served as the gun emplacement proper whereas the horizontal pipe was connected to the base of the upright one and employed as a personnel shelter. This improvisation offered shelter against tanks, could be constructed in a minimum of time, was easy to transport, and highly effective.

In addition to these defensive positions a continuous antitank ditch was constructed which cut across all roads. Temporary bridges, ready for immediate demolition in case of emergency, spanned the ditch where it cut through the roads. Some 18,000 laborers were diverted to the construction of this antitank ditch alone, although they were badly needed to build fortified defensive zones. In order that such zones could be prepared at least in the most essential areas, every man belonging to reserve, service, supply, or headquarters units was assigned his daily quota of obligatory digging that was measured in cubic feet. If necessary the work had to be done at night. To get these positions ready for immediate winter occupancy, the rear echelon units as well as Volkssturm battalions moved into the positions to make the quarters livable. Slit trenches were dug along the roads and antitank and machine gun nests were prepared at all important points. Perimeter defenses were established around every village and hamlet.

The over-all effect of these numerous, fully integrated defense installations was to transform the most vulnerable northeastern part of Germany into one great fortress area. Although some of the defensive positions never played any part in the subsequent fighting, others proved very useful during the battle for East Prussia. If they failed to change the fate of that doomed province, it was due to the entirely insufficient number of troops and to the inadequacy of the weapons which could be mustered for its defense.

Chapter 3

Troop Movements

I. Furlough and Troop Trains under Partisan Attacks

Precautionary measures for the protection of railroads had to be stepped up because of increasing partisan activities in the East. Furlough and troop trains moving over railroad lines which crossed partisan-infested forests were organized as combat units. When a man was sent on furlough he had to carry his rifle until he reached a designated station. He left it there and picked it up on his return trip. The transport commander was simultaneously combat commander, the ranking man in every car was car commander. Demolition of tracks combined with raids from the forests which came close to the lines on both sides were to be expected at all times, particularly at night. In case of a surprise attack or upon a specific alarm signal, the occupants of all cars were instructed to jump off—even-numbered cars to the left, odd-numbered to the right—and to repel the attack. A few assault detachments and a small reserve remained at the disposal of the transport commander in case of a special emergency.

An interesting incident occurred in November 1942 when 6th Panzer Division was moved to the area south of Stalingrad after its rehabilitation in Brittany. The division was loaded on seventy-eight trains of approximately fifty cars each. Each train was organized for combat in accordance with the above-mentioned procedure. Numerous raids and surprise attacks occurred during the trip through the marshy forests. Only a few trains got through the Pripyat region without incident. Most of the attacks were directed against the trains hauling tanks and artillery, and fierce fighting broke out in each instance. One artillery battalion commander and several men were killed and a number of officers and men wounded. The trains were greatly delayed and many of them had to be rerouted. During the ten-day trip they were mixed up and arrived at their destination in improper order and long overdue. A special problem was created by the fact that the trains loaded with artillery and tanks arrived last because twenty such trains were attacked by partisans, some of them repeatedly. This matériel was urgently needed because, from the time when the first train unloaded at Kotelnikovo, the division was under enemy artillery fire and the railroad station was attacked by dismounted cavalry. To secure and enlarge the detraining area required additional fighting. The division had to detrain where the enemy was assembling his forces because there was no continuous German front in this area after the encirclement of Stalingrad. It was due only to enemy hesitation that the units, which had just been unloaded and lacked heavy weapons support, did not get into serious trouble. The enemy started his attack on the assembly area of the completely isolated division immediately after the arrival of the trains carrying the German tanks. On 5 December 1942 an entire Russian cavalry corps with sixty-four tanks drove into the flank of the assembly area south of the Aksay River and achieved a penetration. But during the night the German tanks were unloaded close to the enemy. Some of them were detrained outside of the railroad station and prepared for the counterthrust. On 6 December the bulk of the division with 160 tanks attacked the enemy's flank near Pokhlebin, cut off his retreat, and pushed him against the steep banks of the unfordable Aksay. The Russians suffered a crushing defeat from which only small remnants of the corps and six tanks were able to escape.

II. The Commitment of Furlough Battalions

A few weeks later when the Russians broke through along the Don, the Germans attempted to establish a new front along the Donets River. The situation was serious. The forces available were weak because several armies put in the field by Germany's allies had suddenly collapsed. Every German unit, every German soldier was urgently needed to strengthen the front.

Upon returning from furlough members of units enclosed in the Stalingrad pocket were stopped at Kamensk Shakhtinski on the Donets, assembled, organized into a battalion, and immediately committed along the Donets east of the city. A young first lieutenant was appointed battalion commander and noncommissioned officers commanded the companies. The men came from various units and arms. They did not know their leaders who in turn did not know their men. Equipped with rifles and only a few machine guns, they were to defend a six-mile sector along the river.

The Russians soon spotted this weak sector and, covered by tanks and artillery, crossed the Donets with greatly superior forces and attacked the battalion. They broke through the thinly manned front at various points and advanced swiftly toward the south. The infantry division to which the battalion was attached was involved in heavy defensive battles and could not provide any help. But mobile reserves of the 6th Panzer

Division which held the sector adjacent to the east moved up quickly and attacked the enemy from the rear. Within a few hours the hostile force was destroyed and its remnants captured or shattered. After a few more hours the furlough battalion which had suffered heavy casualties was reassembled. It was immediately disbanded and the men were assigned to their basic arms within the panzer division, where their capacities could again be fully utilized. Every individual member of the furlough battalion was a battle-tested front-line soldier. But hastily assembled in an improvised unit, without the essential heavy weapons, these men could not be utilized in accordance with their abilities. The battalion was doomed in this unequal battle.

The formation of furlough battalions was an unavoidable expedient in critical situations, but it really meant the improper expenditure of good combat soldiers. For this reason furlough battalions had to be dissolved as quickly as possible and the men returned to their original units.

Chapter 4

Combat Arms

I. Infantry

In pursuit, German and enemy forces alike found it expedient to mount on tanks. This improvisation proved effective on innumerable occasions when a defeated enemy was to be pursued. For instance, when 6th Panzer Division spearheaded the drive of Army Group North during the first days of July 1941, it broke through the pillbox-studded Stalin Line after two days of fighting. (Map 1) The enemy offered renewed resistance farther to the northeast but after a few hours the Russians were dislodged from the fortified frontier zone and dispersed into the surrounding forests. In order to take possession of three major bridges before their destruction, it was necessary to prevent the enemy from gaining another foothold. Spearhead panzer units, composed of some fifty tanks with infantry mounted, pursued the retreating Russians relentlessly, occupied the bridges, and—meeting with little resistance—reached the day's objective, the city of Ostrov, within three hours.

Another good example was the battle of annihilation fought southeast of Plavskoye in the Army Group Center sector. It started in the middle of November 1941 when an enemy cavalry division attacked the exposed flank of the army group. Assault guns were to disperse the enemy formations and infantry was to annihilate his forces completely. In order to move the infantry straight into the depth of the battlefield together with the assault guns, volunteers from infantry units mounted the assault guns and, hanging on like grapes on a vine, rode into the enemy lines with all guns ablaze. The enemy cavalry division was obliterated.

In both instances the enemy was totally vanquished and shattered. The completeness of the success of this improvisation can be traced to the panic spread in the enemy ranks by the German tanks. But whenever the enemy was firmly entrenched in front or on the flanks, this venture turned out to be dangerous and costly. During the later years of the war this improvisation was generally discontinued because of heavy casualties caused by antitank weapons and air attacks. Moreover, it was superseded by the introduction of armored personnel carriers.

The Russians also used this expedient repeatedly and found it a fast means of transportation. But whenever they encountered German resistance they always suffered heavy casualties from machine gun fire. For that reason they discontinued this practice when they came close to the German lines.

II. Artillery

In position warfare daily fire direction exercises carried out by the artillery and infantry howitzers assumed great significance. During these exercises all wire and radio communications were prohibited for extended periods. As substitutes field expedients had to be used to maintain communications between observation posts and gun positions. Some of the media employed were signals transmitted by discs, inscriptions on blackboards read with the help of field glasses, mounted messengers, runners, and relayed messages. Much time was devoted to training in Morse code transmission by signal lamps.

Since the German infantry units were usually understrength the Russians were often able to infiltrate through their defense lines. The artillery positions therefore had to be fortified and constructed as strong points in the depth of the defensive zone. The artillerymen had to be given advanced infantry training and were issued extra machine guns and hand grenades whenever possible. The gun crews had to be ready to make counterthrusts which were specified in the combat orders of each battery.

Such a system of strong points proved effective during the summer of 1943 when the Germans were engaged in heavy defensive battles west of Kharkov. The artillery troops intercepted an enemy force which had infiltrated through sunflower fields. For a while the situation looked very critical but the artillerymen, fighting a delaying action, gained sufficient time for the launching of a counterattack which led to the annihilation of the enemy forces.

Some German commands on the Russian front issued orders prohibiting their artillery from firing on enemy command posts. The enemy was to feel secure and was to establish a network of communication lines and observation posts based on his command posts and was not to suffer any interference during that time. But the destruction of uncovered command posts was to be prepared in such a manner that it could be carried out instantaneously in accordance with the demands of the tactical situation. The sudden elimination of enemy command installations never failed to produce a favorable effect on offensive or defensive operations.

Flat trajectory fire from howitzers proved very effective in clearing tree tops in forest fighting. In one instance, during operations near Leningrad in the autumn of 1942, marshy terrain prevented the howitzers from going into position to deliver flat trajectory fire and to assist in the penetration of a large wooded area. The following tactics were therefore employed to cross the wooded region: All artillery pieces, heavy infantry howitzers, antiaircraft guns, and ground support planes were temporarily subordinated to the artillery commander so that he could exercise centralized fire direction. Heavy rolling barrages systematically raked the woods and cleared lanes in one sector after another. For this purpose the wooded zone was divided into 1600-foot squares which, in turn, were subdivided into 400-foot squares. Artillery, infantry, and Luftwaffe units marked identical squares on their maps. According to the attack plan one square after another was raked by heavy concentrations either from front to rear or from rear to front or alternately, but always in conformity with the requests of the assault troops. Smoke shells were interspersed to obstruct the enemy's vision and prevent him from conducting a systematic defense of the forest. The forward assault units were withdrawn a few hundred yards shortly before H Hour to enable the artillery to soften up the enemy positions without endangering the infantry. The delay caused by this withdrawal was made up by the immediate launching of the attack as soon as the fire lifted. During the course of the assault the advancing infantry closely followed each shift of fire, moving into each square as soon as it had been cleared, and proceeded to mop it up.

The detection of German artillery positions by enemy observation was sometimes made more difficult by camouflaging the firing report with the help of an improvised device that simulated detonations. At the beginning of the war most observation battalions were equipped with such simulating devices, but later on only few of them were available and those few were inadequate for actual deception because of the great variety of guns used in counterbattery fire and for infantry support. Actual deception of the enemy artillery observation could only be achieved if the deceptive firing report sounded like the detonation of a real gun both to the enemy ear and to his sound-ranging equipment. A close similarity between the actual and the deceptive report was achieved with the assistance of engineer specialists who built a makeshift detonation device which was thoroughly tested behind the front. The amount of explosives used in this device was regulated in accordance with data provided by the sound-ranging check points. These experiments were continued until the instruments finally showed that the detonations could have originated from 150-mm. field howitzers or 210-mm howitzers. Furthermore it was established that the most effective deception could be achieved by placing the detonation device approximately one mile to the front of the battery which was to be protected but never on its sides or to its rear.

The results of these experiments were confirmed in 1942, when it was necessary to deceive the enemy about the positions and strength of the German artillery in the Volkhov sector of Army Group North. There the 818th Artillery Regiment was faced by numerically superior Russian artillery in extremely narrow positions hemmed in by woods, marshes, and impassable terrain. Deception was essential in order to protect the positions from counterbattery fire and air attacks and to divert the enemy fire by misdirecting it into unoccupied territory. For some time the impact areas of the enemy fire in the immediate vicinity of the detonation devices gave the impression that the improvisation had served its purpose and that the enemy had been deceived, at least for a while. Yet, some caution against overestimating the effect on an alert and well-trained enemy may well be indicated. Although the accuracy of his observation can often be frustrated by distorting the sound patterns. at his control points, the continuous deception of the enemy requires the introduction of a few additional improvisations which might present inconveniences to the artillery units applying them. These are:

a. Several men would have to be permanently assigned to servicing the detonation device and maintaining telephone communications with the gun emplacements. In co-ordinating the simulated detonations to the actual gun reports it is necessary to pay careful attention to the velocity-of-sound factor.

b. The dummy positions must have the outward appearance of fully occupied firing positions. This can be achieved by burning wood fires that leave traces of smoke in the air and show up on air reconnaissance photos.

c. It will be helpful if the camouflage materials are frequently renewed, particularly in the event that tree trunks are supposed to represent guns.

In the field of sound deception, which assumed particular importance when a weak force faced a considerably stronger enemy, several other expedients proved quite effective:

a. Co-ordinating the fire of several batteries or battalions by issuing simultaneous fire commands over the wire or radio fire direction system in order to prevent the enemy from identifying individual emplacements.

   b. Moving individual guns out of the firing positions and including these roving guns in the fire-command system.

   c. Combining a medium battery with a light howitzer battery for simultaneous firing, particularly during the registration fire by sound and flash methods which provided the data for firing for effect, since these preliminaries always took time and were easily observed by the enemy.

Critical ammunition shortages forced the artillery to fire almost exclusively on observed point targets. In view of the circumstances this produced better results than firing on area targets with insufficient ammunition. Harassing fire by sudden concentrations was also excluded. Instead, slow fire by single pieces from many batteries had to be carried out simultaneously according to a precise firing plan. The advantage of this method was that it could be continued all through the night and that enemy communications to the front could thus be seriously hampered and more effectively disrupted than by intermittent concentrations. This expedient was successfully applied at Sevastopol in 1942. According to intercepted radio messages all Russian supply movements had come to a standstill during the nights preceding the German assault.

In many instances the Germans were painfully short of artillery for area targets while the Russians always had plenty of multibarreled rocket launchers and long-range heavy mortars. These were the most suitable weapons to cover an area with surprise fire and to protect flanks.

During position warfare the Germans made up for this deficiency by flexible artillery tactics which included many improvisations. They fired mass concentrations on single point targets when all batteries within range would fire one round. If, for instance, eighty batteries were within range of a target, it would be hit by eighty rounds on one single command. As a result, the individual batteries achieved a maximum concentration on a given area with a minimum expenditure of ammunition. The effect was excellent and this procedure had the additional advantage of frustrating all enemy attempts to detect the location of individual batteries by sound range.

Whenever there was a shortage of antitank guns and whenever defensive sectors were overextended, field howitzers and antiaircraft guns were used as antitank weapons by the Germans. They were emplaced in rear area strong points and were given the mission of stopping at point-blank range all enemy tanks and assault forces which might break through. The field howitzer batteries frequently consisted of only three guns which, however, proved fully sufficient for routine missions particularly when ammunition was in good supply. A Russian cavalry division which had broken through in the 97th Light Infantry Division sector in the winter of 1941 was routed by field-howitzer fire from all directions.

On 26 July 1941 another German infantry division committed its entire artillery regiment for antitank defense against an enemy corps north of Lvov. After the Russians lost a large number of tanks they were no longer in a position to continue the attack. In later years armored break-through attempts repeatedly failed due to the improvised antitank defense system of the artillery. The standing operating procedure for light artillery batteries prescribed that only three guns were assigned to purely artillery missions whereas the fourth was to be employed as antitank weapon.

Although the inaccuracy resulting from wide dispersion made rocket launchers generally unsuitable as antitank weapons, they occasionally proved effective in massed fire. Thus, during the fighting around Minsk in July 1941, an armored thrust launched by the Russians from the woods south of the city was stopped with the assistance of two rocket launcher batteries. In massed fire they scored some direct hits on tanks and succeeded in shooting the turret off one tank.

Massed fire by several rocket launcher battalions against an enemy armored attack echeloned in depth had a particularly strong impact on enemy morale. During the fighting near Voronezh in mid-July 1942 an armored thrust, launched by the Russians from cover of nearby forests, ground to a halt in the face of rocket-launcher fire. Several tanks attempting to infiltrate through gullies were stopped by the fire of some 300-mm. mobile launchers. Particularly in this case the psychological effect was greater than the material damage. The tanks stopped and the crews dismounted and ran away. The other tanks which formed the main spearhead turned back in the face of 320-mm. incendiary rockets. Actually, rocket launchers were not intended for fire on point targets or the destruction of tanks.

III. Combat Engineers as Infantry

When critical situations developed in wide sectors the Germans were often forced to employ combat engineer units as infantry. But this expedient backfired because many essential and almost irreplaceable engineer specialists were lost in combat. This wasteful dissipation of valuable personnel had to be repeated over and over again despite the fact that the responsible commanders were fully aware of its disadvantages. Necessity knows no laws; in critical situations every available man had to be committed at the front. The employment of combat engineers as infantry was very tempting because they were trained for combat and also because they were exceptionally good soldiers. Many commanders were prompted to commit them as infantry when the situation did not fully justify the change. This was all the more regrettable since it was none other than the infantry which had to pay for the improper utilization of the engineers. In extreme emergencies it was of course necessary to use engineer units as infantry. On many occasions the courage and staunchness of the engineers saved the day. For example, when the enemy broke through southwest of Rzhev in 1942, a corps engineer regiment, all engineer units of one division, and even all the construction engineer companies and some of the road-building battalions from the vicinity were committed to stop the Russian thrust into the rear of Ninth Army. The engineers halted the enemy advance and allowed the tactical command sufficient time for countermeasures which eliminated the danger. (Map 1)

PART THREE

IMPROVISATIONS IN THE FIELD OF SUPPLY AND TRANSPORTATION

The German supply and transportation system in Russia was greatly dependent on improvisations because of the peculiarities of terrain and climate. From the outset of the campaign, supply columns were improvised with motor vehicles of every type which had been requisitioned from private owners. They did not fully replace standard military columns since some of the vehicles were in poor condition and therefore of little service. In addition, the problem of replacing spare parts for so many different types of trucks caused incessant difficulties. Yet, most of these vehicles were in service for many years and some of them lasted for the duration of the war.

Chapter 5

Indispensable Expedients

I. The Panje Column

In Russia, motorized transportation was useless many months of the year. During winter and muddy periods the entire supply and transportation system would have been completely paralyzed if supply columns of *Panje* wagons or *Panje* sleighs had not come to the rescue. These vehicles were in use throughout the Russian campaign and were looked upon as vital for the prosecution of the war.

When the German armored and motorized units swept across the dusty plains of Russia during the summer of 1941, nobody paid much attention to the insignificant little peasant horses of the Russian steppe. The tankers and truck drivers could not fail to notice the industrious little animals pulling heavily loaded peasant wagons cross-country whenever they were pushed off the road by the modern mechanical giants. They were looked upon sympathetically, but what was their performance compared to that of the steel colossi and multiton carriers? Any comparison obviously was out of the question. Many a man dismissed them with a disdainful gesture and the words: "A

51

hundred years behind the times." Even next to the heavy cold-blooded draft horses and the tall mounts of the infantry divisions their dwarfish cousins seemed slightly ridiculous and insignificant.

A few months later the *Panje* horse was judged quite differently. It came into sudden demand during the muddy season when no motor vehicle could operate and any number of cold-blooded horses could not move the heavy guns and ammunition. How were the advance elements to be supplied when they were stranded without provisions? By *Panje* columns. Who brought the urgently needed ammunition to the front when the organic divisional supply columns were stuck in the mud as far as fifty miles to the rear of the advance elements? Again the *Panje* column. Who was capable of moving gasoline from the railheads to the mechanical colossi even through the deepest mud? The *Panje* horse. By what means of transportation were the badly wounded to be transported when the most modern ambulances could no longer advance in the mud? The answer was always the *Panje* horse and wagon. From then on they became faithful, indispensable companions of the field forces. In winter the *Panje* horse proved even more essential. The *Panje* sleigh became the universal means of transportation when motor vehicles were incapacitated and roads were snowbound or nonexistent. During the first months of 1942 some panzer divisions had as many as 2,000 *Panje* horses but hardly a single serviceable motor vehicle. For that reason they received the nickname "*Panje* divisions." This unexpected turn of events made the veterinarian the busiest man in any panzer division.

A good idea of the role played by the *Panje* horse may be gathered from an incident which occurred to the 51st Rocket Launcher Regiment when it was moved into the Vitebsk area in January 1942. After having lost most of its vehicles during the battles for Moscow, the regiment was in the midst of reorganization when it was suddenly called upon to participate in the defense against a major enemy break-through at Toropets. The organic prime movers were either unserviceable or had been lost in previous battles. Only a few trucks in poor condition were available. Snowstorms and high snowdrifts at a temperature of $-22°$ F. impeded all motor traffic on the roads. Enemy spearheads were approaching the vicinity of Vitebsk, Velizh, and Velikiye Luki.

In this emergency two rocket launcher batteries were hurriedly mounted on sleighs. Each battery of six 150-mm. launchers was assigned seventy-five *Panje* horses and three ammunition sleighs for each launcher. After they had crossed the frozen Dvina River the two batteries were committed for the relief of Velizh as part of a reinforced corps. Because of the heavy weight of the ammunition — each projectile weighed approximately 110 pounds—the few remaining trucks had to use the Vitebsk-Velizh highway after it had been cleared of snow and mines. During this emergency march the local model of low, small sleighs usually drawn by one or two *Panje* horses proved to be the only effective means of transportation. The large sleighs supplied by the German Army were too heavy and far too wide for the narrow tracks made by native sleighs. Moreover the harness of the *Panje* horses which had to be used in this emergency was suitable for only limited loads. Despite very difficult terrain conditions the rocket launcher batteries reached the city in time to relieve it. On the other hand, four medium howitzers drawn by heavy German horses never reached their destination.

There was not a single German military agency in Russia which was not forced to employ *Panje* vehicles or columns during winter, not even excepting the Luftwaffe. German mechanization had not made sufficient progress to cope with the Russian mud or terrain conditions in winter. As a result German motor vehicles were incapable of replacing native means of transportation despite the fact that the latter were "a century behind the times."

II. The Corduroy Road

War could never have been waged in the vast swamp regions of Russia had they not been made accessible by improvised corduroy roads. These were the most important static improvisation of the entire Russian campaign and many operations in swampy forests and in the mud of northern and central Russia were feasible only because of the construction of such roads. The first corduroy road was built soon after the Germans crossed into European Russia; the last one during the westward retreat across the German border. In the intervening period hundreds of miles of corduroy road had to be built or repaired during the muddy seasons in order to move up supplies and heavy equipment. At the beginning of the war it was often sufficient to construct a cordurory road 25 to 100 yards long to get hundreds of bogged-down vehicles back on the move.

During the thrust on Leningrad in mid-July 1941 an entire panzer corps bogged down in the swampy forests, separating the corps from the Luga River. For several days the corps was unable to assist its hardpressed advanced elements which were surrounded in a bridgehead on the other side of the river. Only corduroy roads built with considerable effort could restore the former mobility of the corps. In another instance, in 1942,

Eleventh Army had to abandon a planned offensive in the direction of the Neva River because corduroy roads could not be built in time.

The swamps along the Volkhov River were impassable because there were no usable roads. The construction of corduroy roads was the only means of overcoming such terrain difficulties. Since Russia lacks rock and gravel but has an abundance of timber in the central and northern parts, the construction of concrete or paved roads was impossible and corduroy roads became the only feasible substitute.

In constructing these roads it was important to select logs about ten inches in diameter and place them in several layers. As in the superstructure of a bridge, stringers, double layers of crossed logs, and siderail lashings had to be used. The guard rails had to be wired because nails could not be used. The cross logs had to be topped with a layer of sand—not dirt—or, when no sand was available, with cinders or rubble. Time and personnel permitting, the top layer of logs was to be levelled off. Only such thoroughly constructed corduroy roads could stand the strain of constant traffic.

The crossing of the many small swamps found along almost any Russian road caused many special difficulties. It was at these points that the supply convoys got stuck when the heavy trucks of the motor transportation regiments sank in. As a result, serious traffic disruptions lasting many hours and sometimes even several days occurred quite frequently. Over and over again the convoy commanders made the same mistake of failing to wait until the roadbed was repaired by the construction of corduroy roads. Instead, they believed that they could force their way through. The flat swampy stretches, which could have been repaired within a relatively short time before they were completely torn up, were soon in such a condition that their restoration became extremely difficult. The road had to be closed to all traffic since it had become impassable and the swampy stretches obstructed the flow of traffic. Frequently repair work could not be undertaken in time because the road construction engineers had no motor transportation and therefore arrived too late at crucial points. In general, the construction of a corduroy road proved sufficient to bridge small swamps. But whenever swamps were too deep a regular bridge had to be built across them.

Corduroy roads had a detrimental effect on the speed of movements since they slowed down traffic. The average march performance of foot troops dropped to two miles an hour whereas motor vehicles could cover about five miles an hour. Traveling along a corduroy road on foot or by motor was very strenuous, and equipment, especially sensitive instruments, suffered from incessant concussions. These roads complicated and slowed urgent movements of reserves in critical situations.

In the Leningrad area there was not a single serviceable hard-surface road leading east toward the German front. (Map 5) In this sector the local army commander was wholly dependent upon two long corduroy roads that covered a total distance of eighty miles. Since they were the only arteries for troop movements and supply traffic, they were used by day and night and their maintenance therefore presented many problems.

In the vicinity of Leningrad two types of construction were commonly used: the heavy corduroy road built over a foundation of five log stringers and the light one which was placed directly on the ground. The two layers of cross logs forming the roadway consisted of logs about five inches in diameter that were secured on both ends by guard rails which in turn were anchored to the ground by drift pins and wire loops. The road was just wide enough for one truck because longer logs could not be procured. Turnouts were built at 1000-yard intervals. Special traffic-regulating detachments directed all movements along these roads.

Chapter 6

Other Expedients

I. Improvisations in the Construction of Bridges

In European Russia temporary bridges were built almost exclusively of wood because iron and steel were scarce. In general, the first construction was a wooden emergency bridge which was not secure against the danger of floods. Later on, this bridge was usually replaced by a permanent structure above flood level. Whenever it was possible, attempts were made to construct double-track bridges. GHQ engineers, bridge-construction engineers, or ordinary construction battalions were usually employed for the building of the first temporary bridges. The bridges above flood level were built by bridge-construction battalions and Organization Todt [*Ed*: paramilitary construction organization of the Nazi Party, auxiliary to the Wehrmacht] personnel. The local civilian population served as auxiliaries and were paid for their services.

During the spring of 1942 one division was ordered to move from Kiev across the Seim River to the east. The floods were assumed to have receded by then, but this was not the case and no bridges above flood level were available. A low emergency bridge had to be quickly constructed. No engineer units were within reach because they were all at the front. There was therefore no other choice but to recall one competent officer and some technicians from the front and to build a 600-foot bridge and a 450-yard corduroy approach road with the help of local civilian labor. The work was completed within five days with the help of 500 women volunteers. These native women were well paid and fed; they performed their heavy work in the best of spirits.

The hauling of the essential lumber and the procurement of nails and iron straps always constituted great problems, mainly because the engineers were chronically short of organic vehicles. Timber-and-nail stringers had to be substituted for the long steel I-beams which were not available.

II. Improvised Road Maintenance

Army and paramilitary construction units were responsible for keeping roads and highways in serviceable condition. This meant hard work and required a lot of manpower, particularly in spring. Special roads were reserved for armored vehicles and maintained with particular care. Along these roads the construction units had to build bridges or fords for heavy tanks and assault guns since the existing ones usually could not carry such heavy loads. These improvised methods of improving the road net facilitated quick movements of entire units and reinforcements which were to be transferred from one sector to another. They contributed decisively to the success of many defensive and offensive operations.

III. Deceptive Supply Movements

Supply vehicles were frequently dispatched along certain routes in order to deceive the enemy and make him believe that these movements meant the relief or arrival of troop units. Dust raised by motor or horse-drawn vehicles behind the front lines also deceived the enemy. The vehicles dragged tree trunks or brushwood along the roads in order to raise more dust.

IV. Invasion Barges as Means of Transportation

During the course of preparations for a landing in England in the late summer of 1940, the Germans built invasion barges, the so-called Siebel ferries, in record time and put them through various tests. These ferries were equipped with four 88-mm. guns and an appropriate number of 20-mm. Flak guns which could be fired at air, land, or naval targets. Powered by obsolete aircraft engines, these ferries reached a speed of four knots. They were actually used for transportation on Lake Ladoga, in the Mediterranean, and in the Straits of Kerch where they performed well.

V. Transportation over Frozen Waterways

Most rivers in European Russia freeze during winter and the ice was frequently used as a roadbed for supply routes. For this purpose the roadway was reinforced by blocks of ice and, whenever the ice grew thinner, by rafts. Such improvised supply routes across and along rivers could be found in all parts of the Russian theater. Leningrad, for instance, was supplied over ice roads during many months of the year and, during the later stage of the siege, even by a railroad that crossed the deeply-frozen Lake Ladoga. The Russians also used their most important inland waterway, the Volga, as a main traffic artery for motor vehicles and sleighs during the winter months.

In East Prussia the entire supply of Fourth Army moved over ice bridges across the Frisches Haff in February 1945. Moreover, during the winter 1944-45, elements of Third Army were supplied with rations, ammunition, and equipment over an ice route across the Kurisches Haff.

VI. Fuel Conservation Expedients

Forced to apply strict conservation measures because of the gasoline shortage, which gradually increased during the war, the Germans introduced wood-gas generators in ever greater numbers. At first these were installed on supply trucks used in the zone of the interior. Fuel conservation measures had to be imposed on combat units soon afterward but the conversion to wood-gas generators was impracticable for tactical reasons. The railroads had to carry all supply as close as possible to the front and were used even for minor local troop movements. In the Tilsit area in East Prussia ration and ammunition trains moved as close as 500 yards behind the front line. On the lower Memel front a narrow-gauge lateral supply railroad was built at 500-yard distance from the main line of resistance.

These measures alone were far from sufficient. The field forces therefore introduced expedients on their own initiative. Every empty truck had to take a second empty in tow. With the exception of certain staff cars no passenger vehicles were allowed to undertake individual trips. Passenger vehicles had to be towed by trucks even during troop movements. These and some other similar measures subsequently became standing operating procedure and their enforcement was strictly supervised. They did not alleviate the over-all gasoline and oil shortage but it was only by their enforcement that it was at all possible to maintain the most essential motor traffic.

VII. Railroad Tank Cars Towed Across the Baltic
(Map 4)

Continuous air attacks during 1944-45 drained Germany's fuel reserves and reduced her means of transportation. The heavy losses of tank cars caused a great shortage of vehicles capable of transporting fuel by rail. Seventy tank cars immobilized in Memel were therefore urgently needed. But it was no longer possible to move them out of Memel because the city was surrounded by Russian forces. Nor were there any suitable vessels on hand that could transport tank cars across the sea. Various expedients were considered in an effort to find a way out but none promised success. Finally an engineer officer calculated that empty tank cars could float on the sea if they were sealed airtight. On-the-spot experiments immediately confirmed this theory. Local naval units instantly received orders to tow all the tank cars from Memel across the Baltic to the nearest port with railroad facilities. Despite all doubts expressed by the Navy, the army commander insisted on the execution of this order. The first vessel with five tank cars in tow arrived in Pillau, west of Koenigsberg, in the fall of 1944 after a night journey of 110 miles across a fairly calm sea. The cars were undamaged upon arrival and were put into service without delay. Thereafter these phantom voyages continued in the same manner night after night with the number of cars in tow varying between eight to ten per convoy. Everything went according to plan. Only toward the end of these curious railroad-sea convoys was it found that several cars had broken loose because of heavy seas and had floated away from their towing vessel. They caused considerable excitement in coastal shipping when they were first discovered and reported as enemy submarines. Naval planes and patrol boats immediately put to sea to observe this enemy threat from closer range. To everyone's relief the dangerous submarines turned out to be the turret-like superstructures of the tank cars which had been lost at night and were now rocking on the high seas. The runaways were soon caught and towed into port.

Chapter 7

Supply by Airlift and Aerial Delivery Containers

I. The First German Experiments

For the Germans, dropping supplies by parachute to encircled units from battalion to army strength had all the characteristics of improvised operations. At the beginning of the first winter in Russia, the Army High Command asked the Luftwaffe to give immediate assistance to isolated or temporarily encircled units by dropping rations, medical supplies, and ammunition in aerial delivery containers which were originally designed for the supply of parachute units in action. In most cases these missions were successfully accomplished in a spirit of unhesitating co-operation between the services.

The need for the first airlift operation arose in 1942, when major elements of Eighteenth Army were trapped in the Demyansk pocket and Hitler ordered that they be supplied by air. The First Air Force was given this mission and assigned three groups of Junkers transport planes as well as some cargo gliders to carry it out. The chief supply officer of the air force formed a special air transport staff which, in co-operation with the responsible army agencies, carried out the supply operations in accordance with requests received from the encircled units.

An adequate airstrip was available within the pocket. The surrounding terrain could be used as a parachute drop zone. The enemy territory to be crossed was narrow and fighter cover was available throughout the flight and during the take-off from the airstrip. There were but few days on which the air lift was interrupted by snow storms, the formation of ice, or fog on the ground. Under such favorable circumstances it was not too difficult to maintain the fighting strength of the encircled forces.

On return flights the carrying capacity of the aircraft was taxed to the utmost since they were loaded with sick and wounded, official and soldiers' mail, and sometimes even with scarce matériel in need of repair. Although few planes were lost through enemy action, the rate of attrition from wear and tear was very high, requiring constant replacement of the transport planes. Because of increased demands by other sectors of the front and the low rate of production, it was even necessary to employ training planes in order to fill the gaps that developed.

In addition to regular airlift operations, aerial delivery containers were dropped by bombers to various isolated units which were in immediate need of supply. In round-the-clock flights the bombers dropped their containers at the lowest possible altitudes despite strongly increased antiaircraft fire. These missions were very costly and put the personnel to a severe test. During February 1942, I Air Corps flew 1,725 bomber sorties in direct support of ground operations and 800 supply missions for the Army; by March the supply missions required 1,104 bomber flights. These figures clearly indicate that great numbers of bombers were diverted from their original purpose and employed in an improvised supply operation.

The Demyansk pocket was eventually relieved and in the opinion of top-level Army experts the air supply operations had been of decisive importance in enabling the encircled forces to hold out.

II. The Stalingrad Airlift

As a result of the above experience Hitler ordered that Sixth Army, which was encircled in Stalingrad during the winter of 1942, be supplied by air. Goering accepted the assignment without opposition although his assistants raised strong objections. The Fourth Air Force was charged with the mission of transporting 500 tons of supplies per day to a suitable airfield near Stalingrad. The experiences of the past winter indicated that only 50 percent of the planes could be fully operational at any given time and that therefore 1,000 transport aircraft carrying an average load of one ton each were required. This calculation did not take into account adverse weather conditions or losses by enemy action. Germany had just about that many transport planes but they were scattered all over Europe. The organizational machinery needed to concentrate most of these planes in the Stalingrad sector, and to improvise the essential procurement and transportation measures, reached truly gigantic proportions.

The circumstances surrounding this venture clearly indicated that it was doomed to failure and Luftwaffe experts therefore seemed extremely skeptical. That their misgivings were justified became obvious when the Russians continued their advance and captured most of the departure airfields within easy reach. As a result many aircraft were lost while they were grounded for repairs. The approach flights led over an ever-widening strip of enemy-held territory which soon extended beyond the range of German fighter cover. Losses in men and matériel were replaced by crews and aircraft from the training commands, so that virtually all training of bomber crews came to a standstill during the winter of 1942-43. By the following spring the Stalingrad airlift accounted for the loss of 240 training crews and 365 training aircraft.   The training program did not recover from the effects of these losses until 1944.

Inclement weather also played its part.   Heavy snowstorms disrupted all air operations for days on end.   Russian fighter and antiaircraft strength increased steadily.   Nevertheless, the German crews did their utmost to accomplish their mission which, however, was far beyond their capabilities.   The amount of supplies which eventually reached Sixth Army was small and could not avert the impending disaster.

Airlift operations in support of entire armies constitute a task which can only be accomplished after careful planning and preparation and then only by an air force which has all the necessary means at its disposal.

Chapter 8

Supply and Transportation Problems
in the Arctic

Most of the supply and transportation problems in the arctic were caused by terrain difficulties, by the virtual absence of routes of communication, by the arctic winter weather with its abundance of snow and ice, and finally by the fact that all sea traffic from Germany to northern Finland was dependent on the navigability of the Baltic. From this arose the need for numerous improvisations.

In the absence of roads that could be used as traffic arteries, the transportation problem could be solved only by the use of very narrow conveyances which could move across open country, through swamps of little depth, and through snow. The ideal means of transportation was the Finnish cart, a narrow two-wheeled vehicle drawn by a small horse. In addition the Germans used self-sprung drag sleds formed of tree forks, which the Finns called *purillas,* pack animals, and human pack bearers. Reindeer served as draft animals during the winter. These reindeer were purchased with the assistance of local experts and given some time to get accustomed to the German soldiers who were to be their new handlers. With its highly developed sense of smell the reindeer does not take to strangers and is likely to run away. For the transitional period of adjustment it was therefore decided to hire the Lapps who had hitherto handled the reindeer. The next step was to train the troops in the handling and care of these animals. In summer the reindeer roam on the open range like any other wild game and can only be classified as such, whereas in winter they become domesticated animals. Even the methods of harnessing and driving reindeer are unusual and must be learned. Each division received one reindeer transport column with fifty reindeer for the primary purpose of facilitating the supply of raiding detachments and reconnaissance patrols. Partly because of foreign exchange considerations the Germans employed relatively few reindeer whereas the Russians organized an entire reindeer division and committed it in midwinter after excuting a major enveloping maneuver on the southern flank of the German arctic front. In this operation the Russian troops and all their equipment were transported on reindeer sleds.

During the unusually severe winter of 1941–42 the Baltic Sea was frozen over for several months and it was not until several weeks afterward that freight traffic was partly restored. Outside the icebound Finnish ports supplies were transshipped to lighters for which a narrow traffic lane could be kept open by a light ice breaker. At times these lighters were unable to come alongside the freighters. In such instances supplies had to be transferred to the lighters over boardwalks laid across the ice. This additional handling had to be taken into account in the packing of supplies at their points of origin.

Supply by airlift was an emergency measure to be employed only when all other means had failed. Under the terrain conditions encountered in the arctic, landings in winter could be made on the frozen surface of lakes, whereas in summer the use of medium and larger-sized land-based aircraft was altogether out of the question. Special crews therefore had to be trained for dropping supplies by parachute. Airlift operations also proved extremely valuable for speeding up the evacuation of wounded from the arctic wilderness.

PART FOUR
TECHNICAL IMPROVISATIONS

Chapter 9

Clothing and Equipment

Improvisations of clothing became necessary when the German Army was suddenly faced with the prospect of a winter campaign in Russia. To alleviate the lack of adequate clothing during the winter of 1941–42, several divisions helped themselves by organizing large sewing workrooms in near-by Russian cities. From used blankets and old clothing, local workers produced flannel waistbands, ear muffs, waistcoats, footcloths, and mittens with separate thumbs and index fingers. Sheepskins were tanned and transformed into coats for sentries and a limited number of felt boots were manufactured in small Russian workshops. It was possible to requisition fur garments and felt boots from local inhabitants for a small number of men. Some winter clothing was also acquired from dead enemy soldiers. Fur-lined coats, warm underwear, gloves, and ear muffs of regular winter issue did not arrive from Germany until the early spring of 1942. During the first crucial winter the available supply was sufficient for only a small percentage of the forces. The clothing of the great majority of men was not nearly adequate since few of them had more than one item of winter clothes. Whoever possessed extra underwear wore one set on top of the other. All supplies of underclothing in the divisional and army dumps were issued. Eventually every man was able to protect his head and ears to some extent by using rags and waistbands.

Effective relief gradually reached the front once the so-called fur collection campaign got under way throughout the Reich. This campaign was by far the greatest and most valuable improvisation in the field of clothing. Even though the outfits were of varied appearance they fulfilled their purpose. If it had been started earlier many casualties could have been prevented during the severe winter of 1941–42.

At the beginning of the war the German armed forces were quite unfamiliar with the geographic data and climatic conditions of the far north. German clothing and equipment allowances failed to take into account the peculiarities of warfare in the arctic. The troop sent to this theater were unable to operate effectively until they were issued the same clothing and equipment as mountain divisions. This consisted of laced mountain boots instead of standard infantry boots, mountain trousers and tunics instead of regular issue, visored mountain caps with turn-down ear and neck protectors instead of the ordinary field caps, and rucksacks in the place of field packs. Every man was issued complete skiing equipment.

Intermediate and lower commands improvised many other items of clothing and equipment but most of them were of little consequence or of limited application and are therefore not mentioned in this study.

Chapter 10

Shelter

The construction of temporary shelters assumed great importance during the fighting in the far north. A lean-to, set against the wind, topped with branches and twigs, served as shelter for raiding detachments in the arctic winter. To obtain heat two logs were split lengthwise, placed on top of one another at the entrance to the shelter, and set afire. This reflecting fire produced sufficient heat even in very low temperatures. In many instances igloos were built and used as emergency shelters. Portable Finnish plywood structures and Swedish canvas tents were provided as semipermanent shelters to protect personnel from the rigors of the arctic winter. Motor vehicles and the recoil fluids in guns were kept from freezing by the use of various kinds of stoves of improvised construction.

Chapter 11

Weapons

There were few improvisations in the field of weapons. The field forces made minor improvements but never went as far as to create new weapons. Captured weapons were not popular with the field forces but frequently had to be used, in order to compensate for German shortages. Captured artillery pieces were organized into batteries and battalions or employed individually. Most of the time they were committed on secondary fronts or in the depth of the battle position as antitank weapons. Their performance was rarely equal to that of German guns. For many of these pieces no firing data were available, others had no sighting devices, and still others were without adequate transportation facilities. Whenever several types of captured guns were assigned to one unit, as in the Crimea and other secondary theaters, the defects and difficulties multiplied in proportion to the variety of types. Lack of ammunition soon put an end to the employment of many of these weapons.

One of the exceptions to the above observations was the Russian heavy mortar which was very popular with the Germans. This weapon was easy to operate, effective, and justly feared. Captured Russian mortars were often organized into batteries and committed at the front with German crews. By request of the field forces, mortars of the same type were produced in Germany in 1944. Even then they could not be issued at all or only in limited quantities because the necessary ammunition was not available at the front.

Painting silhouettes of the most common types of enemy tanks in front view and profile on the shields of artillery and antitank guns proved a very practical antitank defense aid. The vulnerable points were marked in red. In addition there was a warning sign on the shield: "Observe carefully, take good cover, and open fire at a maximum range of 1,000 yards." The distances were indicated by markers on the ground at 200-yard intervals in all directions so that reference points for the exact distance were always available.

As the standard German antitank weapons proved ineffective against the Russian T34, light howitzers as well as captured Russian 76-mm. guns were used as direct-fire weapons against tanks. In addition, hand grenades and mines were produced locally and used as makeshift antitank weapons. During periods of position warfare, the engineers prepared large quantities of wooden-box mines. The bodies were made of impregnated wood and the mines were fired by pressure. The introduction of the *Panzerfaust*—a recoilless antitank grenade and launcher, both expendable—completely superseded previous improvisations in the field of antitank weapons.

Sunflower oil proved excellent for the care of weapons. During the winter of 1941–42 sunflower oil was the only available lubricant which would permit proper functioning of weapons in the cold climate that prevailed on the Russian front. Unfortunately it was produced only in the southern regions and even there not in sufficient quantities.

In general, the existing German weapons were adequate for arctic operations. The need for additional antiaircraft weapons was met by mounting light artillery pieces, barrels pointing upward, on revolving platforms. For operations against Russian raiding parties on the Kandalaksha front, captured Russian tanks were placed on flanged-wheel cars and thus transformed into armored cars on rail. Cross-country mobility was stressed in the choice of weapons but not all requirements could be met. To increase the mobility of the artillery, one pack artillery battalion replaced a field howitzer battalion in each artillery regiment. Later the arctic theater was assigned a recoilless gun battalion. Although this battalion was not nearly so mobile as the pack howitzer units, it was more suitable than ordinary light artillery. Moreover the number of mortars was greatly increased in order to make the infantry more independent of artillery support in difficult terrain. Most rifles issued to the infantry were replaced by submachine guns because the former proved ineffective during combat in the wilderness.

Chapter 12

Technical Training for Arctic Conditions

The improvisation of arctic clothing, equipment, and weapons had to be complemented by special training. The most important objective in this technical training was to make an indefatigable and accomplished skier of every soldier, regardless of where he might be employed. The German training methods deviated from the Finnish since the Finns stressed cross-country skiing. Accustomed to the use of skis as a means of locomotion from their early childhood, the Finns were capable of covering distances of twenty-five to thirty miles a day even during heavy snowstorms. The German skiing technique always emphasized downhill runs. The type of bindings used by the two nations fully expressed the difference between their skiing techniques. Finnish skis merely had a loop to hold the pointed boot whereas the Germans used a regular binding like the Kandahar and mountain boots with toe plates and grooved heels. The Finnish binding did not permit the execution of speed turns while the German binding which had a tight hold on the foot made it impossible to discard the skis instantaneously whenever the tactical situation required it. Although the Finnish method had great advantages in the arctic, where the downhill technique is of little use and where one can easily dispense with speed turns, German skiing instruction continued to follow the Alpine method. The training program included certain theoretical courses such as those on the proper treatment of skis, on the best way to dress in arctic temperatures, and on protecting oneself from frostbite. Special instruction in the handling and firing of weapons by troops on skis played an important part. The training program was standardized throughout the entire theater; it culminated in a field exercise under combat conditions continuing several days and in winter sports competition.

Every replacement assigned to the Kandalaksha front first had to undergo a two-month special training course at Kairala in order to adjust himself to the living and combat conditions of the arctic. The local command had issued explicit directives for this orientation course, including examples of the proper tactics to be employed in the wilderness north of the Arctic Circle. These directives were brought up to date by the inclusion of the most recent tactical lessons, above all in small unit actions. Thus, for instance, pamphlets were issued on the subject of long-distance marches, march security, combat and reconnaissance patrols, outposts, strong points, guard duty, combat intelligence, movement of supply through enemy-infested areas, and operations in snow and ice as well as in primeval forests and swamps.

This type of training was designed to adjust a newcomer to his environment and its peculiar climatic features. Moreover it was to stimulate and further the soldier's natural affinity to primeval forests and vast spaces and to assist him in orienting himself, tracking down the enemy, avoiding ambush, and interpreting footprints and ski tracks. In fact, it was a kind of "Cowboys-and-Indians" training course. Proper attention was devoted to everyday problems such as passing the night in the open in the arctic winter, constructing a brushwood shelter or an igloo, building a reflecting fire out of split logs, finding food in the wilderness, and applying first aid in case of accident or battle injury. A newcomer had to acquire a great deal of knowledge on such subjects before he was qualified to be assigned to a combat unit without jeopardizing himself and his comrades. The numerous field exercises often lasted several days and took place at great distances from the training center. They were conducted under the continuous threat of enemy raids and, almost without noticing it, the novices to arctic warfare became adjusted to the perculiarities of fighting and living in the extreme north. Whenever the combat troops were transferred to quiet sectors, they continued to receive supplementary training which ranged from improving their skiing technique to the proper care of weapons, equipment, clothing, and rations, and included protective measures against frostbite. Courses in the proper treatment of reindeer had to be repeated over and over again in order to prevent the loss of any of these animals which were so difficult to replace. Thus even the experienced combat soldiers in the far north could always acquire additional knowledge.

Chapter 13

Improvised Front-Line Propaganda

During the Russian campaign the Germans made extensive use of frontline propaganda and achieved remarkable results in many cases. The following incident occurred during the winter of 1941-42 when 6th Panzer Division launched a series of limited objective attacks to the west to secure the lines of communication of the German units facing the main Russian assault from the east. (See *Snail Offensive*, p. 7) In this instance, front-line propaganda was improvised very effectively after the second thrust. Among the many wounded and dead Russians collected on the battlefield was Vera, an eighteen-year-old female sergeant. After a few hours treatment for shock, she recoverd from her horrible experience which she compared to the "end of the world." Vera was a medical auxiliary with the battalion that had held the main strong point and had been completely annihilated with the exception of one officer and fourteen enlisted personnel.

During her first days as a prisoner of war she was under a severe emotional strain. Her interrogation confirmed other intelligence on enemy dispositions gathered from statements of other prisoners. By her own admission she was a member of *Komsomol* [Ed: the Russian communist youth organization], that is to say, a convinced Communist. Before she was evacuated with the next transport of prisoners she innocently requested permission to return to her former regiment. Asked for the reason for her request, she replied in a serious and calm tone: "I want to tell my comrades that it is hopeless to fight against such weapons and that the Germans will treat them well. They should come over to the German side." Asked whether she had any other reasons for returning, she answered: "Yes, I would like to save the life of my friend who is still over there." To the question of whether this was not a subterfuge to escape from the Germans, she replied: "No, I have already stated that I shall return and bring along my friend."

Since she could not possibly give away any German secrets and her self-assured statements seemed trustworthy, her request was granted. Dressed in civilian clothes she crossed the German lines at a point opposite the sector held by her former regiment. German scouts escorted her through the deep, snow-covered forest to a place close to the enemy outposts. She promised to return at the same point once her mission was accomplished.

Several days passed but the girl did not return. After twelve days many people expressed doubts as to her true intentions. But on the fourteenth day the designated front sector reported the arrival of two Russian deserters, one of whom was a woman. It was Vera and her companion. Half exhausted from the long march through the deep masses of melting snow, they arrived at the command post. Vera had an interesting story to tell.

After her return to the Russian lines Vera was immediately interrogated by a *Politruk* [*Ed:* low-ranking political officer] who doubted the veracity of her statements when she told him that she had been treated well by the Germans and was able to escape in civilian clothes because of the carelessness of her guards. For five days and nights she was imprisoned in an ice bunker in the company of criminals under sentence of death and was fed bread and water. When she was questioned again she repeated her previous statements. As a result she was returned to her former regiment, given another uniform and assigned to a front-line battalion as a medical auxiliary. This battalion was waiting for the arrival of urgently needed replacements since it had lost its entire manpower with the exception of one lieutenant and a few soldiers. After she was initiated in her duties she took the lieutenant's map and compass and went to the front. There she surprised a Russian sergeant while he was reading a German propaganda leaflet and persuaded him to desert by telling him of her own good experience with the Germans. She talked to a few more men and told them the same story. They believed her and the story spread like wildfire.

One hour after Vera's return to the German lines the remnants of the sergeant's unit consisting of six men and one machine gun arrived at the point where she had crossed and surrendered. They had overheard the conversation between Vera and the sergeant and decided to follow their example. For several days groups of two to three deserters arrived daily at various points along the front. This provided the division with exact information on enemy intentions and facilitated the planning of further attacks.

With regard to the effect of propaganda leaflets dropped from the air, Vera stated that they were hardly ever read by Russian soldiers because such an offense was punishable by death. Moreover the contents were not believed because of the intensive counterpropaganda to which the commissars subjected them. But she was certain that her former comrades would believe anything she wrote in personal letters. Her idea was taken up and soon this valuable correspondence was in full swing. German patrols delivered her hand-written letters at various points in the forest near Russian outposts and attached them to branches in the trees. They were easily recognizable by their red markings. The results were unmistakable since the number of deserters doubled within a short time. When, in addition, her voice was recorded and transmitted over loud speakers near the enemy lines, the number of deserters along the entire sector increased so much that it exceeded 400 only three weeks after the start of this improvised propaganda campaign. This figure was much higher than the combined total of deserters on all other sectors of the entire army front. The idea of using Vera as the mainstay of this propaganda campaign proved very effective.

Four days later a few bottles of liquor made a powerful propaganda improvisation that eliminated the danger of a local enemy penetration. After a German attack with limited objective the enemy attempted several strong counterthrusts. The situation became very tense when several Russian tanks penetrated the German lines and the last reserves had to be committed. The tanks were destroyed but some of the enemy infantry succeeded in infiltrating through the German lines. Not many Russians got through at first but more and more followed. In this difficult situation the local German commander sent a civilian with several bottles of liquor to the Russian soldiers behind his line and invited them to taste these samples. They were told that they could drink to their heart's content if they decided to come over unarmed. Slightly inebriated by the first bottles they began to arrive hesitantly and in small groups without arms. As soon as the first men had convinced themselves that the Germans had no intention of killing them, about fifty additional Russians turned up to receive their liquor. They indulged so heavily that they forgot all about their weapons, quite apart from the fact that they were physically incapable of returning to them. Meanwhile a strong German detachment picked up the abandoned weapons and stopped all further enemy infiltration attempts.

PART FIVE

ORGANIZATIONAL IMPROVISATIONS

Chapter 14

The Manpower Problem

I. The Situation at the Outbreak of War

Improvisations in the field of manpower were rarely necessary as long as the war took a normal course and the nation was capable of providing the men needed for new combat units and as replacements. The situation changed when the manpower reserves at home began to run low and special measures had to be taken to make up for the serious shortage of replacements. Even at the beginning of the war, the Germans had to resort to some organizational improvisations, particularly to strengthen the defenses in the West.

At the outbreak of war in 1939, the frontier defense command of St. Wendel in the Saar was ordered to defend that sector of the West Wall which extended from Mettlach to Saarbruecken. Only a very small force of regular troops was available. It consisted of frontier guard units stationed in the Saar prior to the war. To a frontage of seventy-five miles there were altogether two battalions of medium artillery, with one infantry or machine gun battalion to every twelve miles. Reinforcement by second-wave divisions could not be expected for about fourteen days, whereas first-wave divisions were to be made available later on after the conclusion of the Polish Campaign. The number of available antitank guns and artillery pieces of every caliber was ample but there were no gun crews. To form these crews, conscripts from near-by towns who were in the older age groups were to be drafted directly instead of being inducted through regular channels. No preparations of any kind could be made because the frontier defense command was not notified before mobilization. Consequently quite a few of the men had received different mobilization orders and had already left to join their units. Others had been removed from their homes during the evacuation of those districts of the Saar territory that were closest to the front. Nevertheless, crews for the antitank guns were formed without delay and given hasty two-day instruction urses at their gun positions. Sufficient personnel could be und even for the artillery guns which were organized to ıorm reserve batteries, although the men drafted for this purpose had been trained with entirely different guns.

On the other hand it was impossible to find suitable battery commanders or technical specialists. These reserve batteries were therefore attached to batteries of regular artillery battalions which were part of the frontier defense command. Local border patrol personnel were organized into a regiment with four battalions in order to increase the defensive strength of the infantry and, above all, to obtain personnel acquainted with terrain conditions. Each battalion was assigned to one of the four subsectors along the Saar River. This measure alone amounted to a doubling of the infantry forces and meant the addition of particularly qualified personnel since all the border patrolmen were former noncommissioned officers of the 100,000-man Army.

Even the second-wave divisions activated at the outbreak of the war might be termed improvisations. In addition to a certain number of reservists, many other men had been called up to fill the divisions' ranks. Some of these men had merely undergone a short, eight-week basic training course during the last few years. Others had served during World War I and had never since taken part in any military exercise; their average age was around forty-five. During the winter of 1939–40 the enemy granted the Germans sufficient time for further preparations during which these divisions were consolidated and trained and the men belonging to older age groups were reassigned to service units.

II. The Luftwaffe Field Divisions

The Luftwaffe was still in the development stage when the war began and was experimenting with various forms of aerial warfare. During the course of its operations it was often faced with missions that could only be solved by improvisations. This study describes only those major improvisations in which the Luftwaffe was closely connected with ground operations.

One of the best known Luftwaffe improvisations was the creation of Luftwaffe field divisions. In 1941 the Luftwaffe was at full personnel strength as it was to be greatly expanded after the anticipated rapid conclusion of the Russian campaign. Not only did these plans fail to materialize but, during the winter of 1941–42, the Army was faced with the first major manpower shortage when it ran out of combat troops. On various sectors of the Eastern Front local commanders took the initiative of quickly organizing and committing provisional units composed of Luftwaffe ground personnel, construction battalions, and signal communication units in ground combat. Shoulder to shoulder with Army units, most of them gave a good account of themselves.

As a further step in this direction, Adolf Hitler ordered the transfer of seven divisions from the Luftwaffe to the Army. Goering, the commander in chief of the Luftwaffe, always jealously concerned with his prestige and possibly hoping for a more favorable turn in events, suggested that these divisions remain under the jurisdiction of the Luftwaffe and be subordinated to the Army only in tactical matters. This suggestion was adopted and the Luftwaffe organized ground combat divisions under its own jurisdiction. The personnel of these divisions met with the highest physical standards but the training of the commissioned and noncommissioned officers was totally inadequate for the purposes of ground fighting. The care of weapons and horses left much to be desired. Since the Army was taxed to the utmost, it could provide few instructors and little equipment. Consequently these divisions were sent into combat after receiving only superficial training. They fought as bravely as most other units but their casualty rate was above normal. To the very end of the war, these divisions continued to present a never-ending series of problems to both the Army and the Luftwaffe with the latter obliged to provide a continuous flow of replacements. Time and again the Army had to transfer commissioned and noncommissioned officers to these divisions and provide additional instruction and training so they could serve their purpose.

The consensus is that this improvisation was ineffectual. Despite great devotion and heroism displayed by individual divisions, it would have been preferable to ignore prestige matters and place this valuable personnel at the disposal of the Army without attaching any strings. The policy was not reversed until the last stage of the war when transfers of personnel from the Luftwaffe to the Army finally became unconditional.

III. Maintenance of Combat Efficiency

Delays in the arrival of replacements occurred very early in the Russian campaign. The combat strength of some infantry companies often dropped to an unbearably low level. The first stop-gap measure to be introduced was to screen all supply and service units for men who were fit for front-line duty. When these units were no longer in a position to provide suitable men, others with little or no training were called upon. They were transferred to the infantry as long as they could somehow meet the physical requirements. Since proper training facilities were rarely available, the combat efficiency of the front-line units suffered considerably by the employment of such replacements. Another expedient was to form rifle companies with surplus personnel from artillery, antitank, or armored units that had lost their equipment and to commit them as infantry.

Many artillery and signal units were forced to release commissioned and noncommissioned officer personnel to the infantry and these arms were soon short of technicians and leaders. Any further transfers were therefore out of the question. In such instances the infantry units short of the minimum number of leaders had to be merged. The personnel and training situation of the field forces improved only after each division was assigned its own field replacement training battalion which guaranteed a satisfactory flow of replacements. During position warfare the divisions in the field were then able to raise the training standards by organizing a variety of courses, but the shortage of combat units frequently forced the command to commit these training battalions as temporary combat units. During the last stage of the war, training and replacement divisions of the various armies as well as Army service schools were often called into action in emergencies. As a result, training organizations that had been built up under great difficulties were repeatedly torn apart and destroyed.

Maintaining the combat efficiency of the infantry divisions despite their continuous commitment and the impossibility of relieving entire divisions presented a special problem. When the fighting raged with full fury for several consecutive weeks, it was impossible to relieve the front-line units by reserves because the situation usually was too critical. Only too often the troops were forced to continue fighting until they were completely exhausted. In order to have at least some small but well-rested assault detachment available, the units alternated in withdrawing a small number of soldiers from the thick of the fighting to give them two or three days' rest behind the lines. For the same purpose headquarters and higher echelon supply·personnel up to and including army staffs were committed at the front in rotation.

Since transportation to and from Germany was often disrupted, leaves and furloughs had to be frozen for long periods. Whenever the situation permitted, armies, corps, and divisions therefore established rest camps for the men who were due furloughs. These camps were invaluable in maintaining the combat efficiency and morale of the troops. Another improvisation was the introduction of so-called sponsorships at higher headquarters. Certain staff officers maintained constant personal contact with specific combat units and took them under their wings. Moreover, up to 10 percent of the personnel assigned to headquarters staffs rotated with their comrades at the front to allow them to go on leave or to a rest camp. These measures were of benefit to the troops and improved the relationship between headquarters staffs and combat units.

A very successful improvisation was the introduction of rehabilitation units. Soldiers who had been sentenced to serve extended prison terms but who showed promise of reforming were not relieved of front-line duty but put on parole and transferred to improvised rehabilitation platoons, companies, or battalions. These were committed at critical points of the front. The rehabilitation units had particularly efficient commissioned and noncommissioned officers and gave a good account of themselves. This very effective improvisation soon became a permanent institution which received unanimous approval and was accepted as a good solution not only by the prisoners but also by the officers to whose units they were assigned. In 1944 one of these rehabilitation battalions fought exceptionally well in the encircled fortress of Ternopol in eastern Galicia. When the town fell a number of noncommissioned officers and men of this battalion fought their way back to their own lines under great hazards and hardships.

The organization of indigenous units was another improvisation designed to strengthen German fighting power. Such units were organized in occupied territories and friendly countries, especially by the Waffen-SS [Ed: combat arm of the SS; in effect·a partial duplication of the German Army]. They relieved German units of minor duties and were also frequently committed as combat units. Their performance at the front was far below the standard of German troops. For this reason the front-line troops usually objected to the employment of indigenous units. On the other hand, many volunteers from prisoner-of-war camps were employed as auxiliaries to replace soldiers transferred from supply and service units. In general they were quite dependable and useful.

Late in the war, when few or no replacements were available, all divisions in the field had to use some of their service troops to form emergency alert units. These were originally intended for the defense of strong points or towns in their rear areas or as security detachments for rear positions; but frequently they had to be committed in the front lines to close a gap and sometimes even for the purpose of local counterattacks.

As another emergency measure, convalescent furloughs granted to sick or wounded soldiers were severely curtailed in order to shorten all periods of absence from the front. But, since it was obvious that combat units could only use fully recovered men, most local military authorities failed to comply with these regulations. They also showed great reluctance in carrying out another order which pertained to the induction of men in advanced age groups who were also affeced by the draft because the age limit had been raised. It was felt that these older men ought to remain in their civilian occupations where they would be able to serve the nation much better than as soldiers.

IV. The Employment of Women in the Armed Forces

The employment of women with the German field forces was not as widespread as among enemy armed forces. During the latter part of the war women were used as clerical and signal communication auxiliaries at German forward headquarters. They took over these duties from men who were thereby released for combat. These women soon became familiar with living conditions at the front and settled down to do an excellent job. In the arctic the possibilities for employing women were very limited. In that region army headquarters was the lowest echelon to which the auxiliaries were ever assigned. The Russians on the Kandalaksha front, however, had divisional signal battalions exclusively composed of female personnel. Female radio operators were frequently identified as members of small Russian commando and sabotage teams dropped by parachute in the arctic. Generally these detachments consisted of one female radio operator and eight men.

In Germany proper the program of substituting female for male military personnel met with a great deal of opposition because it ran counter to well-established military traditions. The responsible administrative officials were very hesitant in introducing this new program but as the war progressed the increasing manpower shortage imposed the extensive utilization of women in a variety of military jobs.

One of the first measures was to employ women as instructors at riding and driving schools and as grooms at remount depots. They were also used as maintenance crews for aircraft at training centers, as parachute riggers, and as refueling personnel at airfields. A great number of women were employed as antiaircraft auxiliaries at fixed Flak installations throughout Germany. Toward the end of the war the percentage of female personnel in several searchlight units rose to 90 percent.

The Russians often used women to work as laborers on construction projects. In one instance some women captured near Orel told the story of a Russian improvisation to provide urgently needed laborers for work on fortifications. The impending German advance on Bryansk in 1941 was to be stopped by a strong belt of fortifications at the approaches to the city. For this purpose 100,000 laborers had to be recruited without delay. Among them were women from the Caucasus who had been hotel employees. One day the entire personnel of the hotel were suddenly ordered to assemble in the backyard. Not allowed to return to their rooms, they were marched to the railroad station where a train was waiting to take them to Bryansk. The work on the fortifications around the city took four weeks. At the end of that period all laborers were released on the spot and left to their fate.

The organization of the Finnish *Lottas* shows how the employment of women can raise a country's fighting power by releasing men. The *Lotta-Svaerd*, a sister organization of the Finnish security corps, had a membership of over 100,000 women and girls. During the war they performed all military duties which could possibly be taken over by a woman, regardless of the proximity of the enemy. *Lottas* were encountered in field kitchens of companies in the front lines. The commander of a Finnish border infantry battalion in a very exposed sector of the arctic front used a *Lotta* as battalion clerk and interpreter. The Finns also employed young boys in army uniforms as messengers and for similar duties.

Chapter 15

The Organization of Special Units

I. Staffs

Special command staffs are often needed to carry out certain types of improvisations. A wise commander will anticipate such situations by keeping special staffs at his disposal for any emergency. This is only possible if all staffs not absolutely essential at the front or in rear area assignments are actually pulled out and thereby made available to the command. The Germans might have accomplished a lot more in this respect. For instance, the commander of XXXVI Mountain Corps was under the impression that a corps staff was not needed on the Kandalaksha front and might be put to better use elsewhere. He suggested that a divisional staff with an expanded supply branch would be quite adequate to exercise the tactical command functions in this area. Although he submitted several suggestions along these lines, they were quickly turned down by army. In similar cases it should always be possible to transfer such a staff without delay, if necessary by air, to a point where it might be urgently needed.

In many instances a command staff had to be suddenly improvised to take over some special mission. After the Stalingrad disaster the staff of XI Infantry Corps was reconstituted from an unassigned corps staff which was hastily organized in the beginning of February 1943. Formed in the area north of Kharkov, it consisted of one general and several general staff officers who happened to be in this area on an inspection trip. The staff was to assume command over three German divisions which had been committed to strengthen sectors formerly held by Hungarian and Rumanian forces. These divisions were without higher headquarters after the collapse of Germany's allies on the Stalingrad front. The lower echelons of the staff were picked from the field units, and a Hungarian signal battalion, later replaced by a small German unit, took care of signal communications. The initial difficulties were gradually overcome. It took five months and required numerous reassignments and organizational changes to transform the improvised corps staff into a regular one. Other corps staffs were improvised in a similar manner and their deficiencies were eliminated step by step until they finally became fully organized corps staffs.

In one instance the improvisation of two special traffic regulating staffs made it possible to withdraw ten divisions and thousands of refugees across the Dnepr River. (Map 6) During the course of the large-scale Russian counteroffensive in August-September 1943, the enemy advanced rapidly from the Belgorod area toward Kiev, and Army Group South had to be withdrawn behind the Dnepr. The crossing of the river, which was 2,500–3,500 feet wide in this area, was complicated by the fact that only a few bridges were left standing. Some of the bridges were threatened by the enemy advance while others had been reached by the Russians before the arrival of the German troops. Every possible step had to be taken to delay the enemy advance and simultaneously accelerate the crossing of the German units over the few remaining bridges.

The long wooden bridge at Kremenchug alone had to serve as a crossing point for ten divisions, six of which were panzer divisions. The XI Infantry Corps was put in charge of the river crossing and was assigned two special staffs to assist in this mission. One staff had to make certain that the march order was observed on the north bank and had to enforce one-way traffic in order to ensure a steady flow of approaching units. The other special staff was employed on the south bank of the river at Kryukov with the mission of assuring the rapid debouchment of the divisions. Although the mission sounded simple enough, its execution presented all manner of difficulties. Even before the previously scheduled withdrawal of garrison installations and unwieldy army and army group supply units had been completed, the situation demanded that the panzer divisions cross immediately. Some Russian parachute troops had meanwhile landed on the other side of the river and their ground forces had begun to cross the river upstream. Only motorized units were capable of reaching the south bank of the river between the bridges in time to restore the situation. In order to give the panzer divisions precedence over other units, it was necessary to stop all traffic and clear the roads for the tanks. For five days mixed columns of all arms extending over many miles camped in the adjacent fields or, wherever this was impossible because of the many swamps, they kept to the side of the road and waited for the signal that would allow them to continue on their way. Their campfires were close to their foxholes. Alongside these columns, or trapped between them, were streams of refugees and herds of cattle.

Only radical measures against traffic violators of all kinds made it possible to put the panzer divisions at the head of the columns. Even more difficult than the approach to the 2,500-foot highway bridge was the exit on the south bank because the streets of Kryukov were very narrow and winding. In addition, the drivers had a tendency to slow down once they had reached safety on the south bank or to stop altogether to obtain information on the whereabouts of their parent unit. This had a delaying effect and was therefore very harmful. The attempts of mixed convoys to find the right branch of the road and turn off immediately after crossing the bridge also caused major delays. The drivers seemed to forget that many thousands of vehicles behind them were waiting to cross the river. To overcome this difficulty all units were ordered to continue on the highway to the south for twenty miles from the bridge without regard to resulting detours. Drastic steps had to be taken to enforce this order and many control points and even airplanes had to supervise the flow of traffic.

The two special staffs worked with perfect co-ordination and during the first days directed 5,000 to 7,000 motor vehicles a day across the river. Later this rate was stepped up to an average of 8,000 to 10,000 and within ten days a total of 70,000 motor vehicles had crossed the highway bridge.

Simultaneously, three infantry divisions with their horse-drawn vehicles as well as the trains of two additional infantry divisions crossed the river on a railroad bridge covered with planks. Alongside this bridge engineers built an improvised floating bridge for the crossing of the 30,000 civilian vehicles that were routed through the Kremenchug area during the same period.

The special staffs also regulated the traffic across these two improvised bridges. It was particularly difficult to designate the approach routes to the bridges in such a manner that the columns would not cut across each other or, where that was unavoidable, to establish intersections at points where cross-traffic would cause the least disturbance.

Regulation and control of the river crossing topped all other tactical considerations for ten days. Despite so many difficulties, all divisions crossed successfully with their vehicles and it was even possible to get the slow-moving evacuation transports and various supply columns across the river. The rear guards held out long after the time limit set by army and saw to it that even the last immobilized tanks were moved across the highway bridge. Several tanks were coupled by cables and towed by prime movers although permission for their demolition had been given several days before. At Poltava, twelve freight trains loaded with tanks and other valuable equipment stood ready for demolition because enemy tanks had already cut the railroad track connecting Poltava with Kremenchug. A counterattack by German armor cleared the line sufficiently to allow all twelve trains to pass the threatened points and reach Kremenchug.

The two infantry divisions whose trains had been put across the river at Kremenchug had to cross the Dnepr fifteen miles downstream. Some of the civilian columns and most of the herds of cattle were diverted to that crossing point. None of the engineer units in the area had any standard military bridging equipment, motor boats, pneumatic pontons, or civilian shipping facilities. For this reason the two divisions had to resort to whatever expedients they could devise at the time. The last remaining fishing boats were assembled, floats were built from old logs and native wagons without wheels, and some mill boats anchored along the banks were used as ferries.

With these improvised craft soldiers and civilians were moved across the river with all their equipment and possessions. Wagons that were unsuitable for use as ferries were disassembled, floated across, and reassembled on the south bank. Tied to the various makeshift ferries, the horses swam across without resistance. Herd after herd of cattle was driven into the water, but the animals repeatedly shied away from the 2,500-foot-wide river. Only when led oxen were willing to precede them did the mass of the cattle follow into the river accompanied by shouting peasants crossing in boats on both flanks. Slowly and with deafening roars the cattle waded across the 700 to 1,000-foot-wide shallows. Then they suddenly sank into the navigation channel and with heads up swam silently through the very deep and up to 1,000-foot-wide channel until they could set foot again about 350 to 500 feet before reaching the other bank. Herd after herd, 800 to 1,000 head of cattle each, was driven across the slow-flowing river. Even though some herds had been on the move for a month and had covered distances of 125 to 200 miles, there were no casualties. A total of 64,000 horses and more than 80,000 head of cattle swam the Dnepr. The young animals followed separately on large, boarded-up ferries. This completely improvised measure contributed greatly to relieving the bridges at Kremenchug and proved very effective.

The successful completion of the difficult mission may be attributed to the fact that the dual responsibility for the conduct of operations and for the technical problems of the river crossing was vested in the local corps commander. By this arrangement all tactical and technical measures were coordinated under a single man. But a considerable part of the success is to be credited to the efficient special staffs and to the additional crossing facilities—both major organizational improvisations. Yet all these efforts could have been frustrated had the enemy used strong air forces at the right time. However, they were not effectively committed until 90 percent of the forces had completed the

⸗ossing. Then a Russian bomber scored a direct hit on the detonation device installed on the highway bridge which had been readied for demolition. The charge was set off and the bridge was destroyed. At that time, however, the loss of the bridge was not particularly serious because the rear guard tanks and assault guns were able to withdraw across the railroad bridge which remained intact. Before this attack enemy air activity was negligible, and only one light bomb scored a direct hit on the highway bridge. It merely pierced the surface without damaging the vital bridge structure. The vehicles bypassed the small hole which was covered up within one hour. The flow of traffic was not interrupted.

II. Special Formations

A certain number of the organizational improvisations mentioned in this chapter deserved to be permanently incorporated into the tables of organization and equipment of the units concerned. But only a few were officially adopted because manpower and matériel shortages usually prevented the introduction of far-reaching changes. In order to overcome some of the chronical deficiencies, the infantry corps and divisions were forced to use a number of expedients. When they were on the defensive and had to hold overextended front-line sectors without motorized units, they scraped together all the available motor transportation to have at least one motorized battalion or just one company for emergency purposes. These elements used *Panje* wagons during the muddy season and sleighs during the winter. By this improvisation the command had mobile reserves on hand even though they were small.

The formation of so-called *Korps Abteilungen* [*Ed:* provisional corps] was an emergency measure that was also helpful in deceiving the enemy. Remnants of three divisions which had been badly mauled in difficult extended battles were merged into one division with each of the original divisions forming one regiment. The new division was designated *Korps Abteilung* and distinguished by a letter A, B, C, etc. Each provisional corps carried the corps insignia and each infantry regiment was designated by the number of its former division. The regiments drew their replacements from the Wehrkreis* of their original divisions.

The provisional corps had the combat value of an infantry division and fought equally well. The merger had the advantage that the staffs of two divisions with all their organic units became

---

*Ed: The basic military area in Germany, resembling somewhat the prewar U.S. Corps Area; it had the additional functions of administering conscription policies and furnishing replacements to specific units whose home stations were located in the Wehrkreis.

available for reassignment to new divisions or could be used as special staffs or for some other purpose. On the other hand, the new regiments could not be used as battle-tested cadre for newly-organized units. This disadvantage outweighed all benefits that could be expected from the formation of *Korps Abteilungen*. The field forces resented this measure as well as the policy of giving preference to the organization of new divisions with inadequate cadres instead of providing experienced, though weary, front-line divisions with replacements to restore their former striking power. Whenever a new division without sufficiently experienced cadre was suddenly committed in a major battle in the Eastern theater—as happened only too often—it just melted away like snow in the midday sun. The field forces unanimously requested that the battle-tested divisions be reorganized. Yet, as a rule, new inexperienced divisions were sent to the front despite all the damage caused by this procedure.

The provisional corps may have fulfilled their purpose as a temporary measure, but in the long run they proved to be a handicap rather than an asset. If the purpose of this expedient was to eliminate divisions that had not performed well in combat, it would have been better to dissolve them entirely and not to preserve them in parts.

The German experiments with the employment of task forces were more conclusive. In one instance an improvised task force, organized for a specific purpose, played a decisive role in the annihilation battle near Plavskoye in November 1941. The enemy had moved up an armored brigade, which the Germans were unable to match at that time since their panzer forces were heavily engaged in the vicinity of Tula and no armored units of divisional or brigade strength could be withdrawn from that sector. In this emergency Second Panzer Army entrusted a brigadier general on the staff of XXIV Panzer Corps with the mission of improvising a panzer brigade. Time was of the essence. Discussions with other agencies were no longer feasible and, in any event, they would have been fruitless. For this reason army released some panzer units to the improvised brigade. Equipped with ample authority, the brigade commander succeeded in assembling his force within a few hours. In addition to the panzer units assigned by army, he picked up some motorized artillery and other combat units on his way to the front and brought them along. Other units volunteered to join his task force.

The next day the commitment of the brigade led to a decisive victory. The battle southeast of Plavskoye was won with very heavy casualties to the enemy. Most elements of the improvised brigade could then be returned to their parent units. This example shows that the success of an improvisation greatly depends upon the man who is charged with its execution. Responsible commanders must therefore always keep in mind who is best suited to carry out an improvisation if they want to avoid the mistake of selecting an officer just because he happens to be available. This is of particular importance whenever an improvisation may have decisive influence on the entire situation.

The formation of more or less independent regimental combat teams often became necessary in view of the vastness of European Russia and its terrain conditions. The composition of these teams was usually adapted to local requirements which meant that organized operational units such as divisions had to be split into two or more improvised forces. This measure proved expedient in specific situations which occurred quite frequently in Russia, but was applied only on exceptional occasions because maximum striking power could be assured solely by committing an entire division as one unit. Regimental combat teams were effective whenever they were employed to turn the tide of battle at a decisive point.

A railroad combat team was improvised when the German offensive reached Orel in 1941 and two Russian armored trains were captured intact at the railroad station. One infantry regiment, some artillery, Flak, and railroad engineer elements were loaded on captured railroad trains and attached to the armored trains manned by German crews. This improvised combat team made a thrust to the south in the direction of Kursk and succeeded in surprising the Russians. Within two days the combat team reached Ponyri on the way to Kursk and took firm possession of the railroad lines after some small-scale fighting. Thus the unit contributed materially to the success of an operation which resulted in the capture of Kursk during the muddy period of 1941.

Flying columns were committed for the same purpose as combat teams. In most instances these were motorized units composed of elements from various branches and their strength and structure depended on the mission they were to receive. For instance, in 1941 the 97th Light Infantry Division left its rear elements in the assembly area and improvised a flying column with truck transportation from its service units. This column was composed of three motorized units—one infantry battalion, one artillery battery, and one antitank battalion. By its quick action and deep enveloping maneuvers it spared the follow-up division many casualties.

In another instance a flying column was committed in the Kerch Peninsula immediately after the German break-through of the Parpach Line during the Crimean Campaign. The same evening the column reached the Tartar Wall, a fortified line west of Kerch, and captured the enemy positions. The crucial point for the recapture of the peninsula was thereby once again in German hands. The 132d Infantry Division which followed in the rear could never have reached this point in time.

An interesting improvisation took place in the arctic when a mountain pack bearer battalion was transformed into a mountain infantry battalion. The mountain pack bearer battalion was composed of men in advanced age groups who hailed from the Alps. They were gradually replaced by younger men and the battalion was transformed into a combat unit. Clothing and equipment were appropriate. All members of the unit were experienced skiers but, since they needed specialized training, they were withdrawn from the line for a two-month period. Upon completion of the training this battalion was capable of difficult independent missions in the arctic wilderness.

At the outset of the campaign north of the Arctic Circle it became clear that formations of a special type were required. In the midst of operations, however, any kind of large-scale reorganization was out of the question. As a modest beginning the command decided to experiment with the formation of a swamp battalion which was to be particularly qualified for independent small-unit action in the arctic. Since there was no precedent for the formation of such a unit, it was organized by selecting young soldiers in excellent physical condition who were experienced skiers. They were issued the same clothing and equipment as mountain infantry troops. This proved so effective that all combat troops in the arctic were subsequently equipped in the same manner. A few captured trucks were to provide the battalion with motorized transportation. The men soon gained confidence and adjusted themselves to the difficult conditions prevailing in the arctic wilderness. The Finns provided instructors and gave some welcome assistance. When XXXVI Mountain Corps applied for official recognition of the unit, the request was approved and the battalion was designated a bicycle battalion. A shipment of bicycles promptly arrived; needless to say, they were absolutely useless in the arctic. Following another request the battalion was finally redesignated as an independent motorized infantry battalion. It was issued command cars and *Volkswagen* [*Ed:* the German version of the jeep] which had proved extremely useful in the snow and on the poor, narrow, rocky roads. Now the battalion was truly mobile. Later when the Finnish units which had been attached to corps were pulled out, the new battalion carried out difficult combat and reconnaissance patrols in the arctic virgin forests and barren wastes north of the Arctic Circle.

III. Last-Ditch Improvisations

1. The LEUTHEN Project

When the Russian armies poured across Germany's eastern borders in the beginning of 1945, the Army High Command introduced a major improvisation, the LEUTHEN Project, which constituted a radical change in the Army's replacement and training policy. To the German mind Leuthen, a small town in Silesia where Frederick the Great had won a major battle with improvised forces, was the symbol of a victorious last-ditch stand. It was probably for this reason that the Army selected the term Leuthen to designate this project. The plan foresaw that all training units of the entire replacement army were to be transferred and assigned to the field forces as soon as the code word LEUTHEN was transmitted to them. In immediate proximity of the front these training units were to be subjected to a more realistic combat training than they could possibly receive in the zone of the interior. Moreover, they were to serve as security forces in rear area positions or defense lines. The original idea was therefore both sound and practical, but it should have been put into effect much sooner, when the front was still stable. What actually prompted the execution of the LEUTHEN Project at that late stage, whether it was still the original intention as officially proclaimed or rather the steadily deteriorating situation on the fighting fronts, must be left to conjecture. In reality all the LEUTHEN units were immediately committed and thrown into the thick of fighting in critical situations.

What did the LEUTHEN units look like? In every Wehrkreis there were a number of training and replacement units of various arms which were under the command of division staffs. The men who had completed their training and were ready for combat duty were in the replacement units. The training units were composed of recently inducted recruits who were to be prepared for combat by undergoing an eight-week basic training course. Upon receiving the code word LEUTHEN, the division staffs were to move out with all training units that had completed one to seven weeks of training.

One of the units alerted in this manner was the Special Administrative Division 413 which consisted of several training battalions, a regimental-headquarters, an artillery battalion with an odd assortment of guns, and elements of an engineer and a signal battalion. As a tactical unit, the division was really no more than a reinforced infantry regiment commanded by an elderly general with a small staff. Needless to state, it was absolutely incapable of any combat assignment. The cadre up to the division commander consisted of personnel unfit for combat because of sickness, injury, or for lack of tactical qualifications. Most of the noncommissiond officers had suffered combat injuries of such severity that they were barely fit for garrison duty. Some of the men were entirely untrained, others had completed one half to three quarters of their basic training. Some of them were unarmed because the number of weapons provided for training units did not suffice to arm every soldier. In addition, the various formations had absolutely no organic transportation. There were no more horses than those needed for the normal garrison functions and the division had no field kitchens since the food had always been prepared in the permanent garrison kitchens. The clothing and equipment were equally defective. Quite a few soldiers, for instance, could not be issued garrison belts. In general, everything was in exactly the condition to be expected from a home station in times of stress where shortages have become the rule rather than the exception.

When the LEUTHEN division moved out it was therefore no more than an improvisation of the poorest sort. This might not have mattered so much had the division undergone a rigid training schedule far behind the lines. But even while it was on the approach march to its destination, one of its battalions was shifted from the Main River valley to Hammelburg where a small enemy armored force had broken through. The remainder of the division was immediately sent into combat and annihilated.

In summarizing, one may state that the LEUTHEN Project was doomed from the outset because it was applied in a situation for which it was entirely unsuited.

2. *Other Desperate Measures*

In view of the extremely heavy losses of manpower, the shortage of weapons, and the precarious condition of the transportation system, the situation of the German Army became so critical that the need for improvisations grew even more urgent during the last few weeks of the war. The organizational improvisations of that period were a far cry from those introduced during earlier stages. In many cases the selection and training of replacements was makeshift. Equipment of all types was totally inadequate and consisted of whatever was left over or could be picked up. Since no guns were available, the organization of new artillery units was practically impossible. Whatever new infantry units were organized during this period were of limited capability in the field. In Bavaria, for instance, the last regular activation of a new infantry division took place in November 1944. What followed thereafter was pure improvisation, not so much because of the shortage of trained replacements, but because of the inadequate supply of weapons and equipment.

Although the organization of new divisions had become impossible, replacement units were sent to the front until the beginning of March 1945. Then even this function could no longer be accomplished. Each Wehrkreis assumed command over its replacements, organized a few emergency infantry battalions and transferred them to the nearest tactical command. Many well-trained soldiers were still available but, because of the serious shortage of infantry heavy weapons, it was no longer possible to organize entire machine gun companies. The battalions were therefore composed of a small battalion staff and four rifle companies. Each company had one machine gun platoon with two heavy machine guns and a few locally requisitioned wood-gas-burning trucks, one of which carried a cook stove. The few artillery battalions organized during this period were composed of a great variety of guns. No two batteries were alike and every section had guns of different caliber.

During that period occurred a very significant incident which demonstrated the effects of the improper utilization of administrative personnel. Several first-rate panzer battalions were in the process of rehabilitation at the Grafenwoehr troop training grounds in Bavaria. When enemy armored spearheads approached the area, a corps commander responsible for a near-by sector of the front ordered the staff of the training center to assume the tactical command of the panzer battalions and stop the enemy advance. The commander of the training center was a general well along in years who had always handled administrative assignments very competently but had never during his long career commanded a panzer unit. His staff was composed of elderly reserve officers and ordnance specialists. Their leadership spelled disaster for the panzer battalions.

The numerous organizational improvisations introduced during that period were only stop-gap measures applied in time of extreme emergency. Since most of them were adopted to overcome purely local critical situations they are of little consequence in a study of this type.

Chapter 16

Political Measures Introduced by the National
Socialist Party

I. Civilian Labor Procurement

During the years preceding the outbreak of the war, civilian labor procurement had to be improvised on a large scale for the construction of fortifications. Even at the time when the West Wall was under construction, the allocation of manpower was essentially an improvisation of gigantic proportions. Receiving unusually high pay and enjoying a variety of other benefits, hundreds of thousands of men were employed by the Todt Organization and moved from one building project to the next. Not everything that was built at that time was beyond criticism, yet some of the achievement of the years 1938–39 would not have been possible without these improvisations. Toward the end of the war another improvised labor force was formed to construct additional fortifications in the west. This time it consisted of entire Hitler Youth units, of men who were in age groups subject to labor conscription but too old for military service, and of men who were no longer fit for combat.

The improvisations introduced during that period had highly political aspects. They were directed by laymen some of whom had never seen military service and whose technical knowledge was very limited. They were unaware of the major importance of matériel in military planning and were inclined to confound a temporary surge of enthusiasm—such as undoubtedly existed among the Hitler Youth Combat Units—with real fighting ability. These Party functionaries were under the erroneous impression that their own fanaticism was shared by everybody and that this alone would make up for all the shortages and deficiencies which characterize all last-minute improvisations. On the other hand, there was little opportunity for preventive measures at a time when only painstaking efforts could conceal the existing chaos. The Volkssturm might perhaps have presented such an opportunity if only it had been drawn up as a levee en masse with long-range material preparations and if entirely different slogans had been used for the mental and spiritual conditioning of the people.

II. The Volkssturm

The most extensive improvisation undertaken by the National Socialist Party was the mobilization of the Volkssturm during the last few months of the war. The idea was to call on the last forces of resistance the German people were capable of mustering. A misunderstood and misinterpreted tradition built on memories of 1813 may also have played its part in the minds of some Party officials.

The Volkssturm included all men up to the highest age groups as long as they were capable of bearing arms and were not already serving with the armed forces. This might have provided a broad basis for successfully mobilizing whatever fighting strength had not yet been tapped if there had not been a complete lack of weapons, clothing, and equipment. Whereas clothing and equipment might conceivably be improvised, this does not hold true of arming hundreds of thousands or even millions of men. The Wehrmacht could spare nothing. At the same time it became more and more obvious that the paramilitary Party formations had hoarded and hidden weapons and ammunition, but in view of the large number of Volkssturm draftees these weapons were of little help. Then, a Party official had the idea of manufacturing simplified Volkssturm rifles with barrels he could "procure" from some factories in Saxony. This plan was also of little consequence. Thus the whole project of staging an armed levee en masse was doomed from the very outset.

Leadership and training were two of the other problems to be solved. Among the men of the Volkssturm were many veterans of World War I. Although there had been many changes in the field of tactics, these men had sufficient military background to cope with the simple missions of which the Volkssturm was capable. To provide adequate training was a more difficult matter. Men who differed widely in age, former branch of service, or type of training, as well as men without any training whatsoever, were attending military drill periods in their spare time, as a rule on Sundays. Occasionally, in towns with local garrisons, one or two instructors were provided by regular army units. That was all the assistance the Wehrmacht could give because it had no men to spare. Moreover the Volkssturm was a Party improvisation and probably deliberately kept apart from the Wehrmacht from its initial organization.

Only when actually committed in combat was the Volkssturm to be placed under the tactical control of the Wehrmacht and fight in conjunction with the regular field forces. There was no reason for great expectations. The call to arms for an extended tour of duty was to be locally restricted. The men were to be called upon only if the enemy threatened their home county and even then they were to be used exclusively for local defense. Even that was almost too much to expect. When, toward the end of the war, entire Volkssturm battalions were committed far away from their homes on the Eastern Front, this emergency measure was contrary to the spirit and original mission of the Volkssturm and could only lead to failure.

Guard duty and local security assignments were practically the only missions for which the Volkssturm was really qualified. Its composition, its limited training, and the fact that no more than rifles and in some cases only pistols and hand grenades could be issued as weapons, precluded its commitment in real combat operations. Since it was incapable of withstanding critical situations, the Volkssturm could only become a liability and threat to the troops it was to join in battle. Its proper mission was to construct and guard road blocks. Important psychological considerations spoke against restricting Volkssturm units to purely local commitment. Surely the primary interest of the men resided in inflicting a minimum of war damage to their home towns where their families lived. Thus, it was safe to assume that the Volkssturm men would prefer to avoid any last-ditch stand in the immediate vicinity of their home towns. The tactical commanders therefore took the precaution to suggest that road blocks and fortifications should be erected at a sufficient distance from any community in order to spare it the effects of combat action. Later orders from higher headquarters specified that no Volkssturm units should be committed any closer than thirty miles from their immediate home towns. This, however, meant a complete reversal of the basic principle of restricting the Volkssturm men to the defense of their immediate home territories.

In East Prussia the Volkssturm did a better job than anywhere else. It was there that the idea of the Volkssturm levy had originated since East Prussia was the first German province directly threatened by the enemy. There the organization and training of the Volkssturm made the greatest progress.

East Prussia alone raised thirty-two Volkssturm battalions. All of these remained in that province even when, in November 1944, the civilian population from the northern districts had to be evacuated. After that, most of the Volkssturm units were used to prepare reserve battle positions in the rear area for a possible withdrawal of the combat troops who in turn provided instructors for the Volkssturm battalions. Months of continuous instruction raised their standard of training to such a degree that a number of Volkssturm battalions were able to carry out limited combat missions. A few of these so-called special employment units were equipped with a sufficient number of modern weapons such as the most recent 75-mm. antitank guns, the latest model machine guns, and some older-type small-caliber antiaircraft guns. Some of them even had adequate motor transportation. The units were composed of a small percentage of World War I veterans with the rest about equally divided between 16- and 17-year old youngsters and elderly men from 60 to 75. Some of the battalions were under the command of former staff officers who had distinguished themselves in World War I but were now afflicted with various physical disabilities. The majority of the battalions were short of weapons, equipment, and training, and their employment in actual combat operations was out of the question. It was planned to integrate them into the field forces only in case of a general withdrawal of the lines.

From the outset this was recognized as a serious handicap which, however, could not be corrected since the Army had no jurisdiction over these formations. Time and again the Army requested that the battalions be immediately disbanded and all Volkssturm men fit for combat duty be transferred to the field forces. Yet every one of these requests was flatly rejected by the Party. Thus, during the latter part of January 1945 when the front began to give way, most of the Volkssturm battalions employed in East Prussia were of no use to the Army. Wherever they did not disintegrate altogether, they suffered heavy casualties. But contrary to standing orders, a few battalions had been moved up into combat alongside seasoned field units during the preceding weeks and these battalions gave a good account of themselves. Special mention is due to Volkssturm Battalion Labiau which fought as part of a division improvised from service troops. Three times the battalion was dislodged, but in every instance it succeeded in recapturing its original position by launching counterattacks. In this bitter struggle the battalion commander and most of his troops remained on the field of battle.

At another time the Volkssturm performed less well. Showing much zeal in military matters, Party headquarters in East Prussia produced its own 75-mm. antitank guns with iron-wheeled gun mounts and conducted short training courses to familiarize members of the Volkssturm organization with the weapon. By the end of January 1945 the situation near Tapiau east of Koenigsberg was obscure. (Map 4) There, the personnel of an Army ordnance school was engaged in bitter fighting against advancing enemy armor. The commanding officer of the ordnance school had been killed and Tapiau had changed hands several times but was held by German troops at that moment. Rumor had it that enemy tanks had broken through and were advancing on Koenigsberg. Thereupon Party headquarters improvised an antitank gun battalion with twenty new 75-mm. antitank guns from its training school and dispatched it to the area east of Koenigsberg to take up positions for the protection of that city. At sundown strong armored formations suddenly came into sight opposite the antitank gun position. This impressive spectacle caused such a state of terror among the inexperienced gun crews that they left their guns and ran for cover in all directions. Their leader, a young first lieutenant, tried in vain to stop them. Assisted by a few instructors he succeeded in getting some of the guns ready for action and was just about to open fire when he realized to his surprise that he was facing German tanks. It was the 5th Panzer Division which, after heavy tank fighting in the area east of Tapiau, had succeeded in breaking through the enemy lines and was now assembling in this area in compliance with its orders. For once the failure of an improvisation was of distinct advantage.

III. Paramilitary Units During the Last Stage of the War

Toward the very end of the war the Party organized certain tactical units which were to be committed in the field. Political considerations predominated and outweighed all others. For some time past, elements of the Reich Labor Service had served as antiaircraft units. Since there were absolutely no other forces available, elements of labor service battalions were employed to defend the road blocks they had previously constructed.

Hitler Youth Combat Units, organized during the last weeks of the war, were assigned to the field forces on various sectors of the front. Their special task was the pursuit and destruction of enemy tanks with the help of bazookas and *Panzerfausts*. Just before the end of the war, Party Secretary Bormann attempted to organize an Adolf Hitler Volunteer Corps.

The accomplishments of these various paramilitary units are unknown to the authors.

PART SIX
CONCLUSIONS

Chapter 17

Are Improvisations Inevitable?

A considerable number of the improvisations described in the preceding chapters could undoubtedly have been avoided by normal advance planning. Other improvisations could have been minimized by preparatory measures of a general nature which could have been further developed if and when the need arose. A third category of improvisations could not have been even generally anticipated because they were caused by such abnormal conditions or extraordinary circumstances.

1. Avoidable Improvisations

In an attempt to avoid improvisations one must search for and examine all the problems that may possibly confront an armed force in future wars. First of all it is necessary to determine the probable theaters of war. Nowadays any conflict is likely to assume the proportions of a global war if it transcends the limits of a purely local police action. Prior to World War II the Germans did not think far enough ahead. When, for instance, the Armed Forces Academy needed maps of Finland, it was discovered that the available supply of such maps at the Map Service of the Reich War Ministry was inadequate.

The next step is the acquisition of a thorough knowledge of the potential theaters of war, a knowledge not limited to their broad geographic or military-geographic features, but which includes above all their climatic conditions. In every geographic region the native mode of life is determined by the climatic conditions. For obvious reasons this influence is especially pronounced in the many fields of military activity. Strategy and tactics, organization, weapons, munitions, equipment, clothing, food, training, replacements, billeting, and many other factors are strongly affected.

Moreover, a great deal may be learned in advance about one's potential enemy. Differences between his armed forces and one's own are usually not fortuitous but rather reflect a discrepancy in the military policy of the two nations. The observation of any striking deviations from standard procedures should therefore give rise to speculation about their inherent causes. This will make it possible to decide upon the appropriate measures which must be introduced in every military sphere in case of an armed conflict with that country. Friendly nations which are subject to the same climatic conditions as those of the potential enemy may serve as a source of useful information in peacetime.

Senior commanders in the armed forces and military specialists in all important fields must acquire firsthand knowledge of the climate and terrain as well as the social, economic, political, and military conditions in any potential theater of war or at least in those neutral or friendly countries which show similar characteristics. On the basis of their own observations, these men must determine what is essential for the conduct of military operations. Firsthand personal impressions are indispensable; they may be supplemented by the study of pertinent books and documents and by consultation with private citizens who are likely to have a sound judgment of foreign countries.

Military history is another source of valuable information. It is never too late to determine the reasons for the success or the failure of past operations. Many of the decisive factors have retained their validity throughout the years and their effect on military operations in our time would be very much the same as in the past.

In view of the foregoing, the Germans were in a good position to learn the general as well as the climatic conditions of European Russia and the far north. If they actually acquired this knowledge, the Germans certainly failed to draw the proper conclusions for their military policy. Instead, they were forced to use improvisations because of the lack of advance planning and preparations. If they did not get that information in the first place, they were obviously guilty of neglect. For instance, the Finns might have told them that ordinary flat-country divisions are not suitable for. fighting in the impenetrable forests, the rocky labyrinths, and the swamps and marshes of the arctic. Perhaps German planners were still too deeply entrenched in Central European military traditions. Also, the military were not sufficiently familiar with foreign lands and particularly with countries whose climatic conditions differed from the German. As a result they were lacking in proper personal understanding of what was to be expected. They probably took matters too lightly at the outset. In the field of tactics and logistics in European Russia and the arctic, better preparations might have been made before military operations began. Many improvisations pertaining to tactics and logistics could have been foreseen, in particular those which developed into permanent institutions and were eventually incorporated in German standing operating procedures.

Thus if improvisations ᵢ.re to be avoided, one of the essential prerequisites is the logical application of any knowledge possessed or acquired about a potential theater of war. It may happen that a country becomes involved in a war by surprise; in that event the top-level military leadership must act immediately and take appropriate steps to master the situation. It is wrong to wait until the field forces began to help themselves by introducing improvisations which in some cases may be the wrong ones and difficult to eradicate. After weighing the requirements against the available emergency resources, all spheres of the war effort must immediately be adjusted to the new situation by concerted action. This will prevent many adverse psychological effects which may otherwise easily disrupt the confident relationship between the top-level command and the field forces.

II. Unavoidable Improvisations and their Minimization

A different category of improvisations will be unavoidable whenever an unexpected or unpredictable situation produces the need for extraordinary tactical or logistical measures. A number of the improvisations mentioned in the preceding chapters could not have been avoided, even if adequate preparations had been made. The need arose so suddenly or was so localized that preparations carried out elsewhere could not be used in time to remedy the situation. Logistic preparations, for example, will prove effective only if mobile transportation is readily available in case of a sudden break-down in the movement of supplies. For this purpose higher headquarters may resort to airlift, truck, railroad, or inland water transportation. Such preparations must be made well in advance in order to assure immediate availability of stand-by transportation of the above-mentioned types in sufficient numbers and within reasonable distance.

In situations which require immediate emergency measures there is at first no choice but to improvise extemporaneously. If such improvisations are enforced for some time, it will be possible to correct their deficiencies gradually and to introduce systematic improvements.

Improvisations in the fields of weapons, ammunition, equipment, clothing, or rations can rarely be avoided since it is impossible to anticipate all requirements. In some instances stop-gap measures may well consist of emergency purchases of consumer goods, but a general solution can be found only if the rigid system of standards and specifications adhered to in military procurement can be modified and adjusted to the flexible methods applied by private industry. It would then become possible to provide suitable equipment for specific needs in time, thereby eliminating many improvisations. It goes without saying that one cannot possibly mass produce arctic equipment in peacetime in expectation of an armed conflict in the arctic at some time in the future.

III. Improvisations in Extreme Emergency

In times of extreme emergency, improvisations must be approached from a different point of view and applied with other standards than those used during other periods of the war. In such situations preparatory measures hardly enter the picture because then it is a matter of living from hand to mouth while being catapulted from one crisis to the next. The pressure of time assumes tremendous proportions. Obviously no country at war will ever expect to be faced by a situation such as that with which the Germans had to cope during the closing days of the last war. Much less will any country attempt to prepare for such an emergency.

Chapter 18

The Relative Value of Improvisations

The preceding chapters give a fairly detailed account of German military improvisations and indicate their relative value in a variety of situations. By presenting numerous examples, an attempt has been made to demonstrate why certain improvisations served their purpose whereas others failed. This presentation should enable the reader to draw a number of conclusions that have general validity. The most obvious conclusion is that, because of their always-present inherent defects, improvisations should be avoided altogether whenever possible. On the other hand, some of the improvisations presented in this study were absolutely essential and proved effective. For instance, it would have been absolutely impossible to conduct operations in the arctic or to control the supply situation in the Russian theater, had not improvisations been introduced. That many of them were eventually accepted as standing operating procedures simply ·indicates that they should never have been improvisations. Their success was based on the fact that they were initiated and carried out by experts and that the essential prerequisites for putting them into effect existed in these specific cases.

The failure of any improvisation could be attributed either to the lack of proper planning or to the fact that it had been introduced at a time when the necessary means to implement it were no longer available. In many instances its failure could be traced to the laymen who were charged with the responsibility for its execution. All these factors predominated during the last stage of the war when a great number of improvisations failed to meet expectations.

In general, however, improvisations proved effective provided the right men were selected for their implementation and provided they were enforced with the best available matériel and the firm determination to achieve the intended military purpose.

An observer who looks at the Russian campaign in retrospect will come to the conclusion that the multitude of improvisations which were employed far exceeded what Moltke once designated as a "system of expedients" in the tactical sense. Actually, the Germans were forced to introduce the first improvisations as soon as they crossed the eastern border. The farther they advanced into Russia the more expedients they had to devise. The number rose by leaps and bounds when operations began to be hampered first by mud and swamps and later by snow and ice. During the

last stage of the war, improvisations permeated every compart-
ment of the war effort both within Germany and at the front.
At the culminating point expedients assumed the proportion of an
avalanche, the momentum of which eventually buried the entire
military machine.   Improvisations could never be expected to
compensate for the lack of vision and the fundamental blunders
of German leadership.   It is no exaggeration to state that the
entire Russian campaign will go down in history as one gigantic
improvisation.

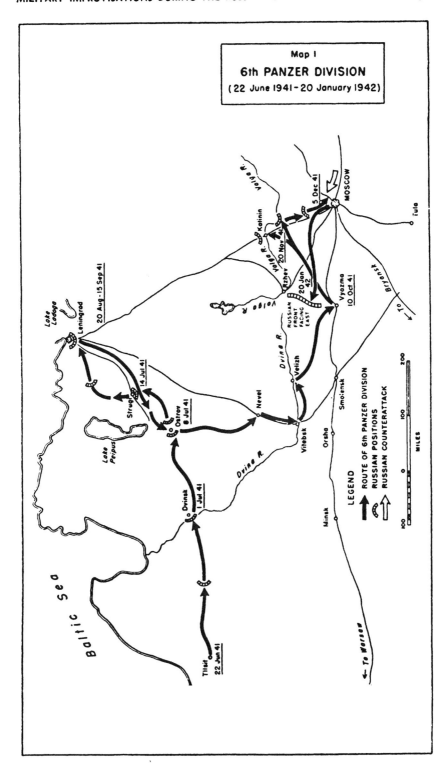

Map I

6th PANZER DIVISION

(22 June 1941 – 20 January 1942)

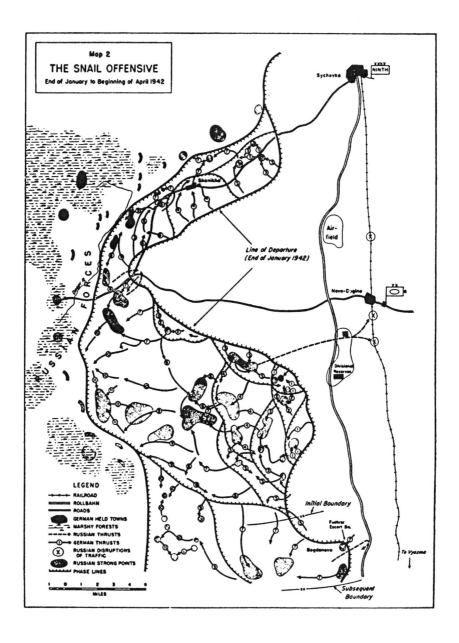

Map 2
THE SNAIL OFFENSIVE
End of January to Beginning of April 1942

Sychevka

NINTH

Line of Departure
(End of January 1942)

Air-
field

Nova-Dugine

Divisional
Reserves

Initial Boundary

Fuehrer
Escort Bn.

Bogdanovo

To Vyazma

Subsequent
Boundary

LEGEND
RAILROAD
ROLLBAHN
ROADS
GERMAN HELD TOWNS
MARSHY FORESTS
RUSSIAN THRUSTS
GERMAN THRUSTS
RUSSIAN DISRUPTIONS
   OF TRAFFIC
RUSSIAN STRONG POINTS
PHASE LINES

1 0 1 2 3 4 5
MILES

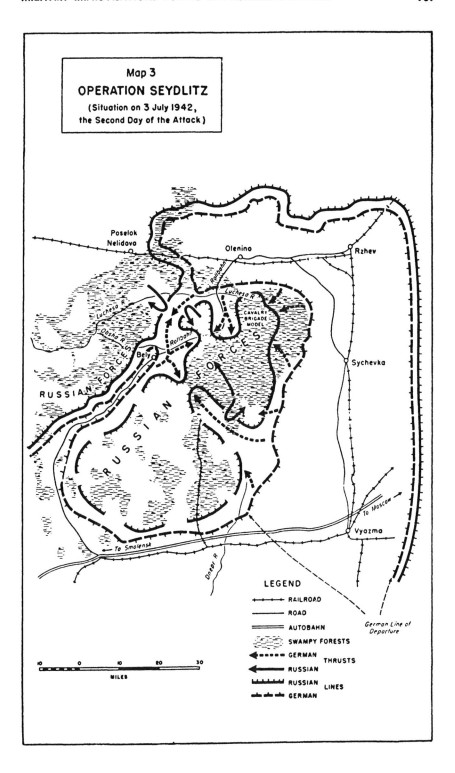

Map 3
OPERATION SEYDLITZ
(Situation on 3 July 1942,
the Second Day of the Attack)

LEGEND

RAILROAD
ROAD
AUTOBAHN
SWAMPY FORESTS
GERMAN THRUSTS
RUSSIAN
RUSSIAN LINES
GERMAN

German Line of Departure

MILES

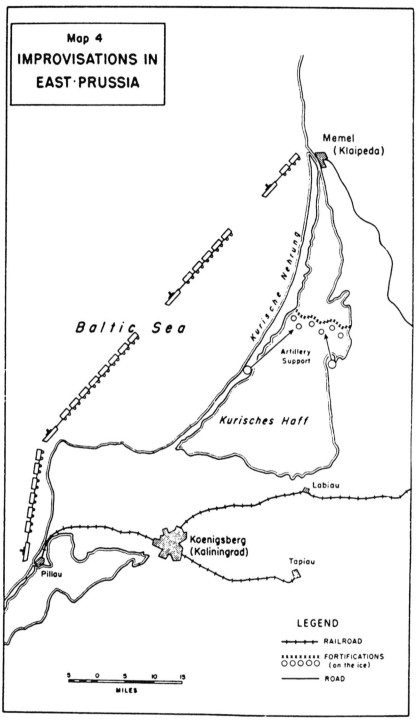

Map 4
IMPROVISATIONS IN
EAST·PRUSSIA

Memel
(Klaipeda)

Kurische Nehrung

Baltic Sea

Artillery
Support

Kurisches Haff

Labiau

Koenigsberg
(Kaliningrad)

Tapiau

Pillau

LEGEND

┼┼┼┼ RAILROAD
xxxxxxxxx FORTIFICATIONS
○○○○○   (on the ice)
──── ROAD

5   0   5   10   15
MILES

804−419−3

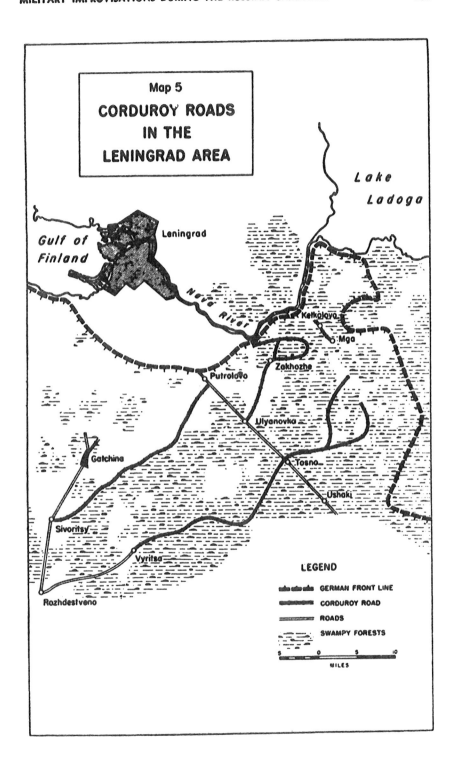

Map 5

**CORDUROY ROADS
IN THE
LENINGRAD AREA**

Lake Ladoga

Gulf of Finland

Leningrad

Neva River

Ketkolovo

Mga

Zakhozhe

Putrolovo

Ulyanovka

Gatchina

Tosno

Ushaki

Sivoritsy

Vyritsa

Rozhdestveno

LEGEND

GERMAN FRONT LINE

CORDUROY ROAD

ROADS

SWAMPY FORESTS

MILES

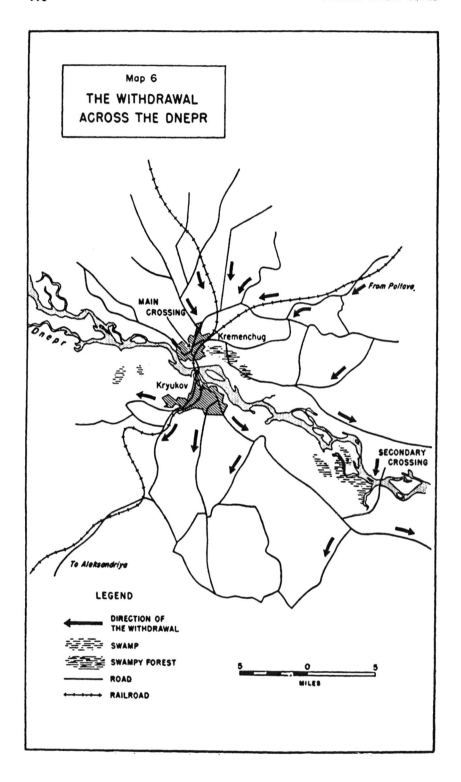

Map 6

THE WITHDRAWAL
ACROSS THE DNEPR

LEGEND

DIRECTION OF
THE WITHDRAWAL

SWAMP

SWAMPY FOREST

ROAD

RAILROAD

Printed in the United Kingdom
by Lightning Source UK Ltd.
136090UK00002B/2/A